# Heart of Abigail

*A LYRIC NOVELLA
OF
JUNEAU, DOUGLAS,
AND
TREADWELL*

## R. Phillip Ritter

*PO Box 221974 Anchorage, Alaska 99522-1974
books@publicationconsultants.com—www.publicationconsultants.com*

ISBN 978-1-59433-102-2
Library of Congress Catalog Card Number: 2009905171

Manufactured in the United States of America.

# Dedicated To:

Kristine Jean Larsen Ritter
who suggested the idea of an historically
accurate fictional story set in Juneau during
the time of the Treadwell mines.

Also by R. Phillip Ritter
*Toil Under the Sun*

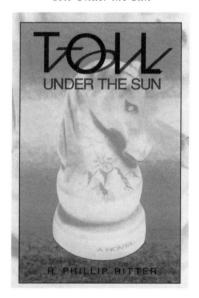

# Table of Contents

# Prelude

*Listen to the voices of the ancients*
*speak to us of Raven and The Old Man.*
*Hear sounds of wind-filled sails and Russian ships*
*and voices shouting sight of Sitka Sound.*
*Mourn long for Vitus Bering's island grave,*
*so near beloved Russia's gentle shores,*
*his life cut short by scurvy's evil spread.*
*Dream of trappers trapping playful otters;*
*of Alexander Baranof who came*
*to Kodiak Island then to Sitka,*
*to build a colony for Czar Paul I.*
*Some years hence he too died upon return,*
*and thus was buried in the icy sea*
*far from the island that would bear his name.*
*Alaska soon ebbed from Russia's int'rest,*
*and so the upstart New World it did buy*
*for an amount thought vastly overpriced.*
*Then prospectors from Wrangell town did spread,*
*and two, Juneau and Harris were their names,*
*guided to find the spot by Chief Kowee*
*discovered what would begin a mad rush*
*to Gastineau Channel to build a town*
*and search for precious gold with hope for wealth*
*and no thought or care of events to come.*

Some believe that people lived in Southeast Alaska in prehistoric times: five-thousand years before Egyptians built the Great Pyramids at Dahshur and Giza; eight-thousand years before Thucydides wrote of Sparta and Athens and the bloody Peloponnesian War in ancient Greece; and nearly ten-thousand years before Russian explorer Captain Alexei Chirikof first sighted the pristine waterways of Sitka Sound in 1741. Farther north, and a day later, Vitus Bering—a Danish-born navigator in the service of the Russian Navy—made landfall at Kayak Island, completing the discovery of Alaska. Bering did not survive beyond the end of the year. Ravaged by scurvy and unable to command his ship, he sailed west past the tip of the Aleutians to the island that would bear his name and there died, six days before Christmas.

Progeny of the prehistoric people, the Tlingit Indians thrived among the islands, fiords, and shores of Southeast Alaska in the days of Chirikof and Bering. Blessed by mild climate, verdant lands, and abundant food, the native peoples carved lofty totem poles with rich designs and built elaborately-decorated ceremonial clan houses and wove spruce roots into baskets and danced and sang and told stories of Raven and the Old Man. They hunted deer, black and brown bear, beaver, and moose. They built fish weirs to trap and then spear salmon upstream. They traveled the waterways in canoes carved from individual logs and propelled by intricately-carved paddles to trade their abundance with other clans. They celebrated births and deaths and marriages and the raising of totems and shared their profit in lavish potlatches. And they viewed the Europeans, newcomers to their ancient land, with both concern and entrepreneurial interest.

The luxuriant fur of the playful sea otter attracted the Russians to return and colonize the Tlingit lands. In 1799 Czar Paul I and his Board of Commerce launched the Russian-American Company and appointed Alexander Baranof as manager and governor of Russian America. Baranof moved the company headquarters from Kodiak Island to Sitka in 1808 and there built a fortified outpost and named it New Archangel. After years of faithful service, and yearning for his homeland, Baranof sailed from Alaska in November 1818, but took ill and was buried at sea in the last days of April 1819.

Forty-eight years hence, in March of 1867, Russia sold the colony to the United States of America—a fledgling land only two years past a bloody Civil War. The price of Alaska?—a mere $7.2 million.

Congress gave jurisdiction of Alaska to the War Department. General Jefferson Davis and U.S. Army troops were dispatched to Sitka and there established a military district. Posts were built in Wrangell and on Tongass Island as well. Military rule of Alaska ended in the summer of 1877 with the transfer of authority to the Treasury Department. The U.S. Customs officer then ruled the land.

A few years before, in the early 1870s, the discovery of gold in the Cassiar District of northern British Columbia transformed Wrangell from military post to boom town. Prospectors traveled from Wrangell to the islands and shores of Southeast Alaska in search of gold, and

two—Joe Juneau and Richard Harris were their names—led to the spot by Chief Kowee of the Auk Tlingits, found precious ore, a hundred pounds or more, in Silver Bow Basin (as Richard Harris called it) on Gastineau Channel on October 4, 1880. Their triumphant arrival in Sitka precipitated a mad dash to Gold Creek, and, without thought beyond the hope of extravagant wealth, the town of Juneau began to emerge. Prospectors also found gold across the Gastineau Channel on Douglas Island, instigating the beginnings of the now famous Treadwell mines.

# Treadwell

*Before the Treadwell mines, arrived French Pete*
*to stake the Paris Lode and Bear's Nest claims,*
*on Douglas Island's eastern-facing shores.*
*But finding low-grade ore (or so he thought)*
*he tried his hand at hawking goods instead.*
*And then upon that fateful day he met*
*John Treadwell, builder from the Golden State,*
*sent by John Fry, a banker, to explore*
*the chance of finding precious gold. And so,*
*John's luck at gold no better than French Pete's,*
*they met and talked of gold and forged a deal*
*that presaged mines on Douglas Island's shores.*
*When an early five-stamp mill proved to all*
*the large-scale promise of the Paris Lode,*
*building the mines of Treadwell forged ahead,*
*with brand new wharfs and chlorination plants,*
*and larger stamp mills to hammer the ore.*
*And buildings for the men who worked the mines*
*sprang up as well: a natatorium,*
*a bowling alley, Turkish bath, a gym,*
*an auditorium—five-hundred seats,*
*a library with fifteen-thousand books.*
*And here my story turns from history*
*to people who thrive only in my mind.*

In May of 1881,[1] French Pete (a French Canadian, his real name Pierre Joseph Erussard) staked the Paris Lode and Bear's Nest claims on Douglas Island. Finding the ore of disappointingly low quality, and in need of a more consistent income, French Pete decided to open a general store instead of developing the claims. In the same year, John Treadwell[2] (a carpenter from California with experience in mining) arrived in Juneau to explore the possibilities on behalf of San Francisco Banker John Fry. John Treadwell staked and explored several claims in Silver Bow Basin, but faring no better than French Pete decided to return home. He packed his bags and waited for the steamship in, as fate would have it, French Pete's general store. After introductions and conversation, and in need of funds to pay for arriving freight, French Pete sold his Paris Lode claim to John Treadwell for $400. He likely thought that he had gotten the best of the deal. The conversation might have gone something like this:

FRENCH PETE: Are you leaving town for good, Monsieur?

TREADWELL: I am, sir. Nothing to keep me here at present. I did my best and now must return.

FRENCH PETE: May I ask, what is your business?

TREADWELL: A carpenter by trade, but here to explore a few mining claims for a San Francisco banker. You see, I've a little experience with placer and lode mining myself. Unfortunately, it did not work out this time.

FRENCH PETE: (*his eyes widening*) Monsieur! I think we do not meet today by a chance! I have staked the claim of Paris Lode on Douglas Island and cannot coax the wealth from it. I would sell it for the price of freight soon to arrive, if you would buy.

TREADWELL (*his pulse quickening*): That's mighty tempting. How much would you ask for it?

FRENCH PETE (*opening a drawer and pulling out a rumpled piece of paper*): I would sell it for…let us say…the four-hundred dollars. Oui, I would sell the Paris Lode for that.

TREADWELL (*after squeezing his chin a few times and gazing for a moment beyond the front door of the general store*): Four-hundred. Four-hundred. Four-hundred dollars. Yes, I will give it one more try. We have a deal, Sir!

The year following this momentous transaction, John Fry, a second partner named James Freeborn, and John Treadwell established the Alaska Mill and Mining Company. Things moved quickly for newly-appointed Superintendent John Treadwell after that. A five-stamp experimental mill, installed in May of 1882, demonstrated the large scale potential of the claim. (An aside is necessary here, and I have decided not to send you to the back of the book to read an end note. In simplified terms, the stamp mill used large iron "hammers" to repeatedly smash the ore to help release the gold. A lot of water is usually required to complete the operation—which explains why a nearby stream could come in handy—as well as screens and amalgamation tables and conveyor belts and whirring cams and dangerous chemicals and other components that only a mining engineer could find interesting. In simpler terms, a five-stamp mill has five "hammers." A 120-stamp mill has 120 "hammers." That's all you really need to know at this point, and all I really care to tell you.) In 1883 men dismantled and removed the five-stamp mill and installed a new 120-stamp mill. In 1884 John Treadwell built a wharf and a chlorination plant. (Alas, another aside is necessary. The stamp mill and its related components only separated some of the gold from the ore. The remaining ore had to be washed and shaken into a concentrate on an inclined belt called a "vanner." Chlorination of this concentrate was one method used to remove the last remnants of gold.) The mill began operating at full capacity during the summer months of 1885, processing 300 tons of ore every day.

The Alaska Mill and Mining Company mill continued to burgeon and change in the ensuing years. More stamps, a matching 120, were added in 1887 to expand the total to 240, making it the largest mill in the world under one roof. In 1889, the recently incorporated Alaska Treadwell Gold Mining Company ("Treadwell Company" from here on) bought out John Treadwell and all other investors for $4,000,000.[3] The Treadwell Company had previously financed two new mining enterprises: the Alaska Mexican Gold Mining Company (incorporated in 1891) and the Alaska United Gold Mining Company (incorporated in 1894). Although the three companies were financially separate, the Treadwell Company managed itself and the other two and played the role of banker. The Alaska Mexican Gold Mining Company emerged 700 feet south of the now substantial community of Treadwell, and began crushing ore with a 60-stamp mill in 1893. The Alaska United Gold Mining Company owned and developed two different properties—the Seven Hundred Foot Mine (not to be confused with the depth of 700 feet: the strip of land containing this mine measured 700 feet wide) and the Ready Bullion—adjacent to and south of the Alaska Mexican Gold Mining Company. If you find this too much to sort out and remember (as I often do), then remember only one thing: the Treadwell Complex (also called the Treadwell Mines) encompassed all that I have described, and sprawled along the shores of Douglas Island beginning one-mile south of the modern day city of Douglas.

Men worked eight-hour shifts in the mines of the Treadwell Complex, 24-hours a day, seven days a week, and every day of the year

save Christmas and the Fourth of July. In return for this brutal schedule of toil, the Treadwell Company made all miners and their families members of the Treadwell Club, with subsequent access to all Treadwell Club buildings and facilities including the gymnasium, natatorium (indoor swimming pool), bowling alley, billiards and pool room, bath and toilet facilities, a Turkish bath (quite popular), a barbershop, a 500-seat auditorium with stage, and a library of more than 15,000 volumes (including the classics) and a reading room of more than 150 magazines and newspapers (including several foreign publications). All-in-all, not a bad existence in those early years.

By 1902 the city of Douglas, initially a residential district for the Treadwell Complex, was incorporated, and by 1908 the city boasted electric street lights, wood-planked streets, schools, and a newspaper. In 1910 the population of Douglas reached 1,722—78 more than Juneau and 500 more than Treadwell. In March of the same year, an explosion deep in the Mexican mine killed 37 miners. Seven years later, in April of 1917, the ground around the natatorium subsided and the rising tides rushed in, flooding the Treadwell, Mexican, and 700 Foot mines.

All of the machinery, horses, and mules were lost in the Treadwell Cave-In; and the Treadwell Complex, in the breadth of a mere four hours, effectively receded into history. But I must stop here, for by reaching beyond the beginning of the new century I have progressed too far. My story begins years earlier, in 1899, during a March month still awaiting the warming kiss of spring.

# Voyage

*Upon its maiden voyage, Willapa,*
*and maiden too, the bonny Abigail,*
*arrived one year before the century's turn,*
*and motoring past Marmion Island*
*at the southern entrance of Gastineau*
*to view the booming mills and wharfs and towns*
*of—south to north in turn—Ready Bullion,*
*Mexican, Seven Hundred Foot, Treadwell;*
*complete with stamp mills, wharfs, and narrow tracks.*
*The day, in early spring, turned gray by clouds*
*scudding low above the snow-crusted peaks*
*of Bradley and Roberts, casting ashen*
*shadows on the wintry streams: Dupont and*
*Nevada Creeks, muddy delta at the*
*mouth of Sheep Creek, with Ready Bullion Creek*
*and Bullion Creek both flowing down from slopes*
*now nude of Sitka Spruce and Hemlock groves.*
*And then, by chance, Miss Abigail did glimpse*
*Treadwell Club, built above the moving tides*
*on sturdy piles, with closely-spaced windows*
*(double-hung); to the south a swimming pool*
*and north the warehouse-clustered Treadwell wharf,*
*and farther north, a half-mile or more, thrived*
*Douglas and the hospital named St. Ann's.*

Bonny Abigail Sinclair, her slender hands sheathed in blackened wool, her swarthy curls tucked neatly beneath a black-wool-red-ribboned Glengarry[4] bonnet, leaned out and caressed the frosty rail at the edge of *Willapa's*[5] bow. The little steamer, the first of the newly formed Alaska Steamship Company, sliced the icy waves of Stevens Passage before steaming past the entrance to Taku Inlet and turning into the southern mouth of Gastineau Channel. Abigail scanned the snow-crusted slopes of Douglas Island, and thought she descried a prancing deer, but then decided not—probably only a gnarled stump. Tiny Marmion Island, at first consumed by the smoothly rising slopes of Douglas Island beyond, broke into clear view as *Willapa* plowed more westerly before turning northwest and tracing a new route down the center of Gastineau Channel.

As the steamer passed Marmion Island and churned deeper into the steel-gray waterway, Mount Bradley, near the center of Douglas Island, and Mount Roberts[6] on the mainland ascended into Abigail's sight. Dupont Creek slid by to starboard, then Nevada Creek to port. She glanced to the right again and studied the silty delta spreading from the mouth of Sheep Creek. Then, swinging her gaze once again to the left, blinked at the randomly denuded slopes of Douglas Island. Where before Sitka Spruce and Hemlock had majestically crowded the rolling slopes, a field of rough-cut stubble now spread hundreds of feet up the mountain in jagged swaths. Ready Bullion Creek appeared, and then Bullion Creek, and, a little more than a half-mile farther on, the edge of Ready Bullion Mine at the southern end of the Treadwell Complex.

"I must say, it is truly amazing." The Captain of the *Willapa*, a man named Larsen born in Minnesota of Norwegian immigrants, leaned over the bow rail next to Abigail. He pressed the mouth of his beloved silver-lined calabash pipe through wind-chapped lips and sucked in a fragrant puff. The bluish smoke gusted through his beard when he exhaled.

"So many trees are gone. Who cut them down?" Abigail rubbed her emerald eyes and blinked again. She squinted to better see the end of a dock jutting 200 feet out into the channel. A cluster of dark buildings, a 400 foot open pit invisible below, swarmed around the foot of the dock.

Captain Larsen adjusted the brim of his captain's hat and coughed. "Miners cut the trees down…to build Treadwell…and to warm themselves in winter. Started nearly 20 years ago and haven't stopped yet. Probably never will." The faithful *Willapa* churned through a gentle swell and splashed ragged foams of icy water across the bow. "That first dock is for the Ready Bullion Mine. You can see the 120-stamp mill just beyond. They built it about a year ago."[7]

The *Willapa* motored on. Abigail eyed another clump of structures, a little more than 500 feet north of the Ready Bullion mill. "And what is that next group of buildings, Captain Larsen. Is that also part of the Ready Bullion, as you call it?"

"No, Miss Abigail. That's the Mexican Mine. That steep-roofed building sticking out over the water on pilings with the walkway all round is the new boarding house, and a bit further is the mill—the miners enlarged it to 120 stamps six years ago.

The *Willapa* motored on. Abigail tugged her Glengarry down against the biting cold of a sunless day. Moisture-ripe clouds streaked the northern skies beyond Mount Roberts and Juneau. "And I see train tracks. Where does the train travel, so far out here in the wilderness?"

"It goes all the way from one end to the other of the Treadwell Complex, south to north, connecting the Ready Bullion, Mexican, 700 Foot, and Treadwell. Snakes out to the wharfs and up the hills too—connects just about everything, I would say."

The *Willapa* motored on. Abigail gracefully wiped a drop from the tip of her nose with a gloved finger. Her green eyes studied the tallness of the receding hoist building, then followed rumpled mounds of crushed ore down to the mill. Just north of the mill, hanging out above the water on piling like the Mexican Boarding House, she spotted a sleek gable-roofed building with horizontal wood siding and closely spaced double-hung windows. She pointed. "Captain, that building does not have the look of a mill or a mine to it. Do you know what it is?"

Captain Larsen allowed himself a brief chuckle before resuming his pipe. "Yes, miss. That's the Treadwell Club,[8] and there's swimming in that building to the south. They've got a first class billiards and pool room at the club, and a library too. I've played a game or two there myself. Up the hill is the 240-stamp mill, and just north of the wharf is the power plant, 300-stamp mill, and vanner room. They finished the 300-stamp mill this year, and I heard it's the largest in the world.[9] Hard to believe that you'd find it here, but it's actually true."

The *Willapa* motored on. As they passed the massive Treadwell

Wharf—the great dock laden with warehouses and narrow gage tracks and equipment and iron-ringed barrels and piled supplies of all sorts—a handful of salty mariners plied the decks of a two-masted schooner and yelled and heaved lines. A little more than a half-mile farther north, Abigail spotted another jutting dock. She waved north and then rested her hand on top of the Glengarry. "Is that another mine, Captain?"

Captain Larsen squinted toward the distant dock. "No miss. That's the town of Douglas. The tracks run there too, to the sawmill I believe. That's where the St. Ann's Hospital[10] is too, where you'll be

working. By the way, miss, if you don't mind my asking, but ain't you a bit young to be a nurse?"

Abigail's lips curled ever so slightly. "Dear Captain, twenty-seven is not young, and I can assure you that my travels from Edinburgh to London and then to Toronto, Seattle, Victoria, Ketchikan, Sitka, and now this cold and foreboding land have hardened my maturity beyond any perceived deficit of years."

"Yes, miss. I believe you, and I'd reckon that should come in handy if you're going to survive this place." Captain Larsen glanced at his watch. "Better get below now and pack your bags. We dock in Juneau in half an hour."

"My bags are already packed and waiting in my stateroom. I will stay here at the bow of your ship if you don't mind, so that I can properly observe the city of Juneau when we arrive."

"I guess you could call it a city of sorts. It's been a pleasure miss. Now I've got a few things to get done before we arrive."

The *Willapa* motored on.

# Arrival

*As Willapa first touched the Juneau quay,*
*and Abigail did stand upon the prow,*
*at first to glimpse the fledgling Juneau town—*
*by now two decades minus two years old—*
*her eyes instead did sight the brawny form*
*of blondish youth, his tasseled hair uncombed*
*and wearing the Sinclair Red, a pea coat*
*purchased in Seattle with meager funds—*
*all that he could afford, if truth be know.*
*His name, Erik Meyer, she soon would learn,*
*sent by F.W. Bradley, of Treadwell fame*
*and also of Idaho's Coeur d'Alene,*
*to fetch her (and her steamer trunk as well)*
*and drive her in a muddy one-horse cart*
*to the Juneau Hotel, recently built*
*between the local paper and saloon.*
*She worried that the noise would prove too much,*
*but Erik told her not to worry such,*
*for Treadwell ran all day and through the night*
*and he slept well except on Christmas Day*
*when mining stopped and eerie silence held*
*and broke his sleep with silence-caused unrest.*
*And now the story really moves along,*
*for Abigail's true love has now arrived.*

Lanky, muscular, authentic, blonde-mop-haired Erik Meyer grunted and shoved a 327-pound wood-framed packing crate across the rough dock boards to clear the way. Sailors hauled the *Willapa's* bow line taught as the little steamer gently nudged the splintered wharf edge. A lumpy iceberg meandered peacefully near the centerline of Gastineau Channel. Erik studied the glistening chunk of glacier before swinging his gaze across the *Willapa's* bow. His eyes drifted past the Glengarry bonnet then snap-returned. Beneath the red-ribboned cap, her green eyes peering back into his, fair Abigail Sinclair leaned over the bow rail and breathed in the coolness of the salt-scented morning breeze. Erik jerked his head away and pretended to study the iceberg again, but did not see it.

Abigail leaned against the *Willapa's* bow rail to improve her sight as she watched the sinewy young man throw a prodigious wooden crate clear of the falling gangway. She noted with keen interest that he wore a double-breasted wool pea coat of Sinclair Red Tartan, and that he probably had not combed or brushed his sandy hair for days, or more likely weeks from the look of it. Their eyes met for a moment, then the young man appeared to look for something out in the gray waters of the channel. Abigail stepped away from her post at the bow and walked to the gangway. When she arrived at the bottom, the young man surprised her with a haltingly formal greeting.

Erik bowed just enough to see Abigail's brown-polished shoes beneath the hem of her wool dress, and kept his hands out of his pockets as he had been instructed. "Good day...morning to you, ma'am. I'm supposing you must be Miss, Miss Abigail...from Toronto...Canada?"

Abigail smiled, but only slightly. "I suppose you would be supposing correctly then. And what might your name be, and how do you know me?"

"Ma'am, Mr. F.W. Bradley[11] sent me down to the dock to fetch you, and told me to keep my hands out of...to bow when I greeted you, like a proper gentleman. Mr. Bradley is one of the engineers at Treadwell. Everyone likes him real well." A collar of heat stretched around Erik's neck; he stuck both hands in his coat pockets.

Abigail smiled more broadly this time. *Yes, that is definitely the ancient Sinclair Red Tartan. But where did he get it? He is surely not a man of Scotland.* "Might I ask where you found the coat you're wearing? The material is familiar to me, and brings fond memories of home."

Erik recalled J.W. Bradley's admonition to avoid putting his hands in his pockets and abruptly yanked them out. "The coat, ma'am?"

"Yes, the coat."

"I bought the coat in Seattle, ma'am, the day before I boarded the steamer to Juneau. Lucky for me that I liked the color—it was the only coat in the store that I had money enough to buy."

"I like the color too." Abigail slid her fingers beneath the lapel above Erik's heart and squeezed. "Are you here to help with my luggage as well? I brought a heavy trunk, but I have seen that you easily have the brawn to deal with it."

Erik trembled at Abigail's brief touch. "Yes, ma'am, and I brought a wagon to haul it." Erik turned and pointed at a mud-covered one-

horse delivery wagon just off the end of the wharf. "I was told to take you to the Juneau Hotel for tonight. You will be moved to the place you will stay tomorrow."

"And where is this Juneau Hotel?"

"It's right between the newspaper and saloon, ma'am, not far from here."[12]

Abigail frowned, but Erik did not notice. "How lovely. I hope the saloon is not too noisy at night."

"Oh, it is not noisy at all like the mills at Treadwell. They run all the time and make so much noise. But after a while, you get used to it. I only wake up now when they stop on Christmas day. I will fetch your trunk and we can go there now. In the morning, I will pick you up and take you to your quarters at Treadwell. We will have to catch the ferry, so I pick you up at around eight o'clock."

"And is there somewhere I can find breakfast before we leave in the morning?"

"We can get something to eat after we cross the channel. They have good food at Treadwell."

Erik Meyer trotted along the side of the *Willapa* and turned sharply up the gangway. He vanished for nearly a minute before reappearing with Abigail's canvas-covered steamer trunk slung across his back. He bounced awkwardly down the gangway, almost falling off twice, and nearly knocked Abigail to the ground as he rushed by her with the swaying bulk of the massive trunk. Abigail stepped deftly aside and watched Erik weave dangerously between men working the wharf and miners and sailors and stacked crates and barrels and piles of supplies covered with canvas tarps and iron mining equipment and some things that she couldn't identify as he worked his way toward the wagon. He tossed the trunk onto the wagon bed with a crushing thump and then looked back at Abigail, still standing on the wharf next to the steamer *Willapa*.

Erik waved. "Come. I give you a ride to the hotel, so you don't have to walk."

Abigail sighed and began trudging to the mud-covered one-horse delivery wagon and Erik Meyer. When she arrived at the front of the wagon, Erik had already hopped into the seat and was waiting patiently.

Abigail climbed into the seat next to him and smoothed her dress. Erik snapped the reigns and clicked his tongue, and the wagon lurched ahead, nearly throwing Abigail into the wagon bed.

# Quarters

*Flosie, a little ferry of southeast,*
*built to traverse all routes of Gastineau,*
*and steer around small glaciers floating by,*
*did transport Abigail and canvas trunk*
*from Juneau to the Treadwell Complex wharf*
*in eighteen-ninety-nine, the month of March,*
*with Erik at her side to lead the way*
*to her new home in Douglas by the tracks.*
*Upon arrival at the Treadwell wharf,*
*Abigail, with help from Erik's brawny hand,*
*alighted on a narrow flatcar bed*
*and sat upon her trunk, the only seat,*
*to ride the miners' train to quarters new.*
*From Treadwell wharf the tracks of narrow-gage*
*arced to the north and rattled through a switch,*
*passed below the smoldering power plant*
*and echoed train noise off the vanner room*
*(why they call it a "room" I cannot say)—*
*clamoring steel wheels on steel tracks—*
*to pass beyond the Treadwell Complex edge*
*and head for Douglas, half-mile more or less.*
*The churning locomotive slowed at last*
*not far enough from Abigail's front door*
*and Abigail then soughed—you'll learn the word.*

The 72-foot ferry *Flosie*[13] steered clear of the Juneau dock and veered southerly toward the Treadwell Complex. Abigail seized her customary position near the bow, a pair of rusty anchor chains hampering ideal proximity. Erik Meyer secured her canvas-covered steamer trunk in the passenger cabin amidships before joining her at the narrow prow of the sleek little steamer. He tripped on a deck cleat but, to his surprise, adroitly regained full balance to avoid slamming into Abigail's back. She turned at the noise of the stumble, but too late to see the mishap. Seeing nothing, she returned her gaze above the ship's bow. Resting on the distant peak of Mount Bradley, gray-streaked clouds hovered momentarily before a renewed gust from the southeast sent them rolling along the ridge line in tattered disarray.

"Did you sleep fine at the hotel, ma'am? I hope it was not too noisy for you." With both hands Erik crushed a wool newsboy cap into an unidentifiable gob in front of his silver belt buckle.

A few seconds passed before Abigail spoke. "So Erik, did you come from Germany originally? You have a bit of accent."

Erik responded with unforeseen embarrassment. He turned the cap over and crumpled it some more. "Yes ma'am. My parents came to America when I was twelve, but after we arrived they allowed me only to speak English. I grew up in the north of Germany, near the boarder of Denmark.

Abigail realized her mistake just as she spoke the words. "I meant no insult, Erik. I like a bit of accent. It gives you the lilt of sincerity. And, you may have noticed, I have a bit of accent myself, so we are much the same."

The *Flosie* slowed, maneuvered cleanly around an iceberg, then accelerated as it returned to course. Erik's hands relaxed a bit and the cap expanded to partial shape. "Yes, ma'am."

"You may call me Abigail, Erik. I believe we have known each other long enough."

Erik glanced down at one of the rusty anchor chains, then returned his gaze to Abigail's emerald eyes. "Yes, Miss Abigail."

Abigail soughed.[14] "I guess that will have to do for now, Mister Erik."

Erik decided to change the direction of the conversation. "Look, Miss Abigail—you can see the Treadwell dock is near." He pointed vigorously to make sure she didn't miss it.

Abigail studied the intricate dock, bristling with blackened piling, cluttered with warehouse buildings and other paraphernalia of the mining industry. "That's quite a sight. It looks like it is meant more for provisions than people."

"I have seen it work for both, Miss Abigail."

The *Flosie* slowed and maneuvered to the side of the dock. Dirty men in dark clothing tossed frayed hemp lines across oil-glistened water and over the *Flosie's* starboard gunwale. The *Flosie's* deck crew reeled the lines in efficiently and tied the ferry off to the Treadwell Dock.

Erik bowed and straightened his cap out before jamming it on his head. "I get your trunk now, and we go ashore." Erik vanished into the passenger cabin. A few seconds later he appeared astern of the cabin before forcing himself and the bulky canvas-covered steamer trunk up and onto the dock with an impressive groan.

Abigail stepped over the gunwale with the help of one of the deck hands. He tipped his hat as their hands touched. She positioned herself several steps away from Erik to avoid injury from the swinging trunk. "Now tell me Erik. Do we ride another one-horse wagon to my quarters?"

Erik swung the trunk around—as Abigail had predicted—and frowned. "No Miss Abigail. We take the train.[15] The tracks run from the dock right by your new place. I load your trunk and we get started." Abigail followed Erik down the wharf to a pair of dead-ended narrow gage tracks. Steam billowed around a small locomotive pulling two flatcars. Men had already piled both of the flatcars with barrels and boxes and coils of rope and other gear. Erik said something to one of the men then handed the trunk to him. Erik sat on the edge of the flatcar, stood, then bent down and offered his hand to Abigail. "I help you up Miss Abigail. It is a big step for someone of your size."

Abigail reached out her hand, but was not prepared for what happened next. Erik squeezed his fingers around her wrist and hoisted her up to the bed of the flatcar in a rapid swinging motion. When her feet slapped the wooden boards Erik immediately released her hand. Abigail wavered, spun around, wavered again, then regained her balance. She felt her head, then looked down on the dock. The Glengarry rolled around against the edge of the polished rail.

For the first time, Erik observed Abigail's lovely dark curls, then quickly followed the gaze of her eyes down to the track. "Oh, Miss Abigail—you have lost your pretty hat! I fetch it for you." Erik leaped off the flatcar and landed inches from the wayward hat, nearly stepping on it. After snatching it up he rubbed it briskly along the sleeve of his Sinclair Red pea coat and offered it up to Abigail. "I think it's good as new, Miss Abigail."

Abigail accepted the hat with a smile "It's alright Erik. The wind must have caught it. It's alright." She adjusted the Glengarry to a proper slant before plopping down on top of her trunk.

The wheels of the locomotive squealed steel-on-steel and the flatcar shuddered. Erik quickly slid along the edge of the bed, swung his legs around, and stood next to the canvas-covered steamer trunk as the train pulled away.

"It is a good thing I saw your hat, Miss Abigail. We might have left it there."

"Yes, Erik. Thank you."

The locomotive and heavily-loaded flatcars rumbled down the narrow gage track along the north side of a long warehouse to a juncture of dark wharf and dark land.

"How far is it, Erik?"

"Not far, Miss Abigail. Your new place is in Douglas, less than a mile from here. It should take only a few minutes to reach it."

The train followed a smoothly engineered arc northwesterly and rattled through a switch before speeding by a blackened-immensely-cylindrical oil tank and the smoldering Treadwell power plant.

"Where do you live, Erik? Do you have a place in Douglas, too?"

"No, Miss Abigail. I live in the boarding house,[16] south of Treadwell wharf. We didn't go that way. We can go there to get breakfast after you settle in your new place and I move the trunk."

A little farther on, the metallic whir of steel wheels echoed rhythmically off the Treadwell vanner room and 300-stamp mill in quick staccato pulses. The locomotive pushed on, clusters of little wood houses dotting the hillside, then travelled through an open area before arriving at the edge of Douglas.

"Is that Douglas, Erik?"

"Yes Miss Abigail. That is Douglas and you will be staying in one of those houses."

The train slowed to a stop less than 10 feet in front of a row of one-story gable-roofed dwellings, stacked closely together and nearly touching. Abigail stood, and Erik shoved the canvas-covered steamer trunk to the edge of the flatcar bed before dropping down to the snow-mud-crusted ground. He quickly turned and offered his hand to Abigail.

"Are you planning to yank me down to the ground, Mister Erik?"

"No, Miss Abigail. I help you jump down." Erik squeezed Abigail's fingertips as she stepped down, then pulled the trunk off the flatcar to the ground in one smooth motion. Erik waved at the locomotive and the train pulled away from Abigail's new quarters. Erik lifted the trunk again, opened the front door with his free hand, and banged the ungainly trunk against both jambs as he stepped into the little wood house. He quickly popped back out and smiled. "Well, Miss Abigail, you are now home."

Abigail studied the little house, the rough-hewn horizontal wood siding, the steeply-pitched-metal-sheathed gable roof, the pair of double-hung windows spattered with frozen mud, the mounds of dirty snow piled around the wood stoop below the front door, and the train-burnished narrow-gage rails tarnished gray by the reflected wintry sky. Abigail soughed. "Yes, Erik—I can see that I am."

# Lessons

*Three weeks of time had passed since they first met,*
*and on a blust'ry day of rain-drenched winds*
*at good day's end of toiling at St. Ann's,*
*and trudging down the trail to her new home*
*she was surprised at Erik sitting there*
*on her stoop, with a little box nearby.*
*A gift he'd brought, of something dear to him,*
*to trade for lessons, if she would agree.*
*Dancing lessons, that's what he said he sought,*
*and he knew that Miss Abigail could teach*
*him to dance, because that is what he hoped,*
*so he could ask a Miss Marie Prideaux*
*to dance with him, and not appear the fool.*
*She took the box and quickly looked inside*
*to find a gentle feline, Smokey named.*
*At first she refused the gift, then obliged*
*and agreed to meet—Treadwell Club at eight.*
*The graceful waltz, the polka, and two-step*
*were the only dances that he must learn*
*and two weeks remained to fulfill the task.*
*This first dance lesson, go well it did not,*
*so Abigail decided they should meet*
*each night till the approaching dance commenced*
*and maybe then he'd have a petite chance.*

Three weeks and a day from arrival, on a late April afternoon of rain-fragrant blustery southeast winds, Abigail stepped off the end of the boardwalk and maneuvered along the muddy path that led to her quarters by the tracks. Weary from a long day of useful work at St. Ann's Hospital, she thought of supper and a cup of hot tea. As she reached eyesight of her front stoop, a red plaid jacket and newsboy hat came into view, the wearer squatting on the stoop next to a small box. *That looks like Erik. But I haven't seen him in three weeks or more—not since breakfast. What business could he have with me now? I can't imagine after so long.* Abigail quickened her pace for twenty strides then slowed and clasped her hands behind her back as she approached Erik and the small box.

Erik spotted Abigail and stood awkwardly. He nodded politely, and began crushing the wool hat to signal Abigail's appearance. "Good evening to you, Miss Abigail."

Abigail stopped in front of Erik, pressed her feet firmly together, and reclasped her hands in front. "Good evening to you too, Mr. Erik. I haven't seen you for quite awhile—more than three weeks, I would guess. What have you been about?"

Erik looked down at Abigail's toes. "Mostly working in Treadwell mine, Miss Abigail. I haven't had the time to come visit."

"Oh, I see—not that I was expecting you. And what might you have in that box that you've brought with you, Erik?"

Erik bent down and lifted the box. Something rustled inside. "I have something to ask of you, Miss Abigail, and I thought I should give you something in return."

Abigail brightened. "And what is it you have to ask of me that deserves a gift?"

"There's a big dance planned at the Treadwell Club, in two weeks…"

"Yes."

"And I don't know how to dance…"

"Yes."

"And I thought that you might be willing to teach me to dance…"

"Yes."

"Because I'm guessing you know how…

"Yes."

"And I wouldn't feel right asking Miss Marie Prideaux to dance with me…"

Abigail paused. "Oh, I see."

"If I don't know how. I'm hoping you can teach me in exchange for this gift." Erik pushed the box against Abigail's arms. "Your gift's inside." Abigail placed her hands underneath the little box. Just as she did, something moved inside. "Oh my, Erik. What is it that you have inside that moves so?"

Erik smiled broadly. "It's my cat, Miss Abigail. His name is Smokey, and he lives with me at the boarding house, in this box—he likes boxes—but I thought you might want to keep him here instead so that you will not be lonely. I think Smokey will like it here too because I am gone so much. All he needs is his box and he will stay here, and I know you will take good care of him."

Abigail sniffed. "Erik, I cannot accept your cat. The gift's too much."

"No, Miss Abigail, I want you to keep him. He's a gentle animal, and doesn't make much noise, and after you take him maybe you would agree to teach me to dance?"

Abigail did not feel that she could refuse the gift. She opened the top of the box and Smokey poked his soft black head out and trilled. "Erik, he's a lovely creature. Thank you."

Erik relaxed his grip on the wool cap. "You are welcome, Miss Abigail. And now can you teach me to dance so that I am not the fool with Miss Marie?"

Abigail sniffed. "Yes, Erik, I can teach you to dance so that you are not the fool with Miss Marie. And when would you like to start?"

Erik wedged the newsboy hat on. "The Treadwell Club has space after dinner tonight. Could you give me dance lesson tonight, at eight?"

Abigail thought about a cup of tea and supper. "Yes, Erik. And what should I do with Smokey in the meantime?"

"I will set his box inside your quarters. He will like the spot next to your bed. Then we let him outside so he can catch a mouse for his dinner. Maybe he catches two. He is a good mouser."

———

Erik and Abigail stood facing each other in the empty Treadwell Club Auditorium. Abigail tried to blot Miss Marie Prideaux from her thoughts. She had a few ideas other than blotting as well.

After a minute or more had passed, Erik queried, "Miss Abigail?"

The empty room lined with chairs returned to Abigail's sight. "Yes, Erik. I was just thinking of which dance we should start with. Do you know what kind of music they'll be playing?"

Erik pulled a rumpled shred of paper from his plaid coat pocket. "I made some notes, Miss Abigail, from the poster. The waltz, the two-step, the polka—these are the dances I must know."

"Have you tried any of them, Erik?"

"My mother try to teach me to waltz, when I was a boy, but I do not think I remember much."

"That holds some promise. We will start with the waltz then. Now, before you try some steps, you should remember that the music for the waltz will have a three count pattern to it, like this—" Abigail danced the woman's part without Erik and counted out loud, "… one-two-three-one-two-three-one-two…" as she spun in graceful swirls beyond Erik's reach. She stopped in front of him again with her hands on her hips. "Does that make sense to you, Erik?"

"Yes, Miss Abigail."

"Now, the way we hold each other is very important." Abigail stepped close to Erik and looked up at his chin. She grabbed both of his hands. "Now, your right hand goes around my back, like this, and your left hand holds my right hand, like this." She placed her left hand on Erik's shoulder.

"How long do we stay this way, Miss Abigail?"

"For the whole dance, Erik. Now, the next thing you do is take a step forward with your left foot."

Erik abruptly pulled Abigail tight against his chest, slid his leg wildly forward into the folds of her dress, and lifted her off the floor—he stopped still holding her in the air crushed together with his leg stuck out.

Abigail gasped without sound at the squeeze. "Erik—you put me down right now!"

Erik released his grip and dropped Abigail to the floor. "Yes, Miss Abigail."

Abigail brushed the front of her dress to straighten imaginary wrinkles. "Erik, I think we are going to need more than one lesson. How much time did you say we have until the dance?"

"We have two weeks, Miss Abigail."

"Only two weeks? Well, I suppose that will have to do. I think we should meet here every evening until the night of the dance. It's the only chance you have. Are you willing to do that, Erik?"

"Yes, Miss Abigail." Erik looked down at the floor. "Miss Abigail—do you promise I will be ready to dance with Miss Marie Prideaux?"

Abigail soughed, reached out and touched Erik's lowered chin, and raised his eyes to her's. "Yes Mister Erik, I promise you will be ready to dance with Miss Marie Prideaux."

# Dance

*Vainglorious Ulrich Boucher, butcher—*
*that is what it means, the origin, French,*
*and to a blood-thirsty man it belongs.*
*But our villain is not so transparent,*
*for shrouded in appearance debonair*
*he presents grace and sophistication*
*to the eyes of those lacking discernment.*
*But far worse, he has a taste for Marie,*
*and cannot extract her from deep inside*
*the dark and concealed bowels of his mind*
*where vanity and avarice compete*
*for dominance of twisted desires.*
*Wretched Marie Prideaux, once attracted*
*to Ulrich Boucher because of his charm,*
*cannot escape his eternal pursuit*
*and regrets the sad moment they first met,*
*but now too late, and nothing to be done.*
*Into the grasping claws of this drama*
*innocent Erik Meyer blunders in*
*seeking a simple dance, or so he thought,*
*and by chance unleashing the evil wrath*
*of the charming butcher—Ulrich Boucher.*
*Now the novella takes a tragic turn,*
*as, I suspect, you believed that it would.*

Suave, arrogant, guileful, pathologically-self-centered Ulrich Boucher fidgeted near the main doors to the Treadwell Club Auditorium. He stroked his overly-manicured mustache and finely-trimmed goatee and dart-glanced around the room, now quickly filling with people—mostly miners. The Treadwell Band adjusted music stands and prepared to warm up on the garland-festooned stage.[17]

"She's not here, boss." Ulrich's chief lackey, an inconsequential but devious man named Kearney, ground his teeth on a toothpick. "Probably outside flirting with one of the miners."

Ulrich leaned forward, his hand curved over the hound's head ivory handle of his gentleman's umbrella. Manufactured to his personal specifications in St. Etienne, France, the umbrella concealed a rapier fencing blade with an unusual feature: the blade craftsman had sharpened only the last two inches of the tip to a razor edge for cutting. "My good man, I can see for myself that she is not here merely by looking around the room. A woman of her great beauty is impossible to miss. And as for your unproven accusation, any man would consider himself favored of the gods to win the attention, no matter how ephemeral, of Marie Prideaux."

Abigail and Erik, who at Erik's insistence had arrived much too early, stood across the room near a row of chairs. Erik fidgeted too, but for a different reason. "What should I say to her to make her dance with me, Miss Abigail?"

Attempting to appear cheerful, Abigail smiled weakly. "First, Erik, wait until the band plays a waltz. I am convinced that it is much too dangerous for you to attempt a polka or two-step. Then you walk right up to her with confidence, look her right in the eyes, bow like I showed you, and ask her, 'May I have this dance?'"

Erik rubbed sweat off the back of his neck and wiped it on the front of his shirt. "I bow and say may I have the dance?"

"No Erik—may I have *this* dance. And remember not to talk about yourself, and especially mining. She probably hears too much of that kind of talk as it is. Ask her questions about what she has been doing this week, and the like."

"I ask her questions about what she has done this week. Yes, I remember."

"So what kind of question do you think you might ask her?"

"I can ask her if she has enjoyed the weather this week, or if she has not."

"That's not a bad question, Erik, except it's been raining and blowing like a banshee all week."

"Then should I ask her if she has missed the sun?"

The band ran slowly up and down a B-flat major scale, then double-tongued the same scale a little faster.

"That's not bad either, Erik, but maybe you should just ask her if she's done anything interesting and let her do the talking. That'll give you time to think. But don't think so much that you forget to listen."

Miss Marie Prideaux entered the room with graceful strides and flowing gown, heels clicking provocatively on the wood floor. When she neared Ulrich, he sidestepped in front of her to block her path and then bowed audaciously.

"Good evening Miss Prideaux. I have been waiting ever so expectantly for you, all the while agonizing as to why you refused my gracious offer to escort you to this lackluster affair of boorish miners."

Miss Marie Prideaux recoiled. "I explained to you before Ulrich. I'm not interested in your advances at the present time."

Ulrich smiled a sly smile and squinted slightly. "Yes, Miss Prideaux, you did not fail to make that clear, but I would be remiss if I did not offer you the chance to rectify your error."

"There's nothing to rectify, Ulrich. I am not interested in your company tonight. Now, if you would kindly step out of my way so that I can participate in this—what did you call it?—this lackluster affair of boorish miners."

In a fateful stroke of dreadful luck, the Treadwell Club Band began playing the Blue Danube Waltz, and Erik, twisting his sleeve from Abigail's grip, charged across the auditorium floor to ask Miss Marie to dance. When he arrived, Kearney blocked his way. Too focused on his goal to think rationally, Erik lifted the little man up and set him aside before stepping up to Marie and Ulrich.

"May I have this dance, Miss Prideaux?"

Ulrich jerked his head around and quickly evaluated the tall man looming by his side. "And now, behold, one of the boorish louts deigns to speak to us. Do us a favor big man, and begone."

Erik glanced quizzically at Ulrich then spoke directly to Marie a second time. "Miss Marie, may I have this dance?"

Marie glared at Ulrich as she answered Erik's question. "Why yes, Mister Meyer, I would love to dance. Erik bowed again and grinned at his shoes.

Ulrich tasted a burst of rabid bile at the back of his tongue. "Do not dance with this ill-mannered rube, Marie. I forbid you!"

Marie glared a second time. "Forbid all you want Ulrich, but I will dance with Mister Meyer."

Erik grabbed Marie's softly curved fingers and pulled her away. "We must start dancing now Miss Marie, before the waltz is finished."

Marie, keeping her eyes fixed on Ulrich's spiteful gaze, spun around into Erik's arms and commenced dancing. This surprised Erik at first, but he quickly found his stride as they moved to the center of the floor. The Treadwell Club Band began playing the waltz in earnest, with the bass and snare drums emphasizing the beat *boom-tatt-tatt-boom-tatt-tatt.*

After three successful rotations, Erik relaxed a little and remembered his instructions from Abigail. "Have you done anything interesting this week, Miss Marie Prideaux?"

"Why Erik, I'm surprised that you would ask such a thing."

Erik blushed. "Did I not ask the right question? I can ask a different one."

"No, Erik. It's a lovely question. No man I know would care to ask of *my* interests. They only care to talk of their own. I'm touched."

"Thank you, Miss Marie." Erik decided to try a second question. "And have you enjoyed the weather this week?"

Marie smiled. "Have I enjoyed the weather this week? The rain and wind—is that what you mean?"

Erik frowned then remembered that Abigail had told him not to ask this question. "No, Miss Marie. I mean, I…you have not told me of your interesting week yet."

"Oh, I see. Well then, shall we forget the dreadful weather and get back to my interesting week?"

"Yes, Miss Marie. That is what we should do."

The Treadwell Club Band exuberantly wrapped up the final measures fortissimo and the waltz ended. The auditorium exploded in applause to celebrate the first dance of the night.

"You dance beautifully, Erik. Where did you learn to dance the waltz so well."

Erik paused before answering. He detested lying, but could not help himself. "My mother taught me, when I was a boy."

"Well, Erik, you certainly must have been an attentive student. Would you like to dance again?"

"Only if they play the waltz. I only dance waltz. I do not dance two-step or polka."

Marie nodded. "I see, a true man of culture. Then we shall wait until the band plays a waltz, and we shall dance again. Is that acceptable to you, Erik?"

"Yes, I will ask you to dance with me when they play waltz again."

"Erik, you may ask me to dance every waltz tonight."

"Thank you, Miss Marie. I will."

Malignant, seething, wrathful, narcissistic Ulrich Boucher glared at Erik Meyer and squeezed his fists. "Kearney—"

"Yes, boss?"

"I want you to keep an eye on this Meyer fellow."

"No problem."

"We may have to do something about this bothersome interloper."

Kearney grinned and chewed his toothpick. "Just say the word."

# Summer

*The grand Fourth of July, one of two days*
*each year that silenced the toil of the mines,*
*the other (surely you've guessed) Christmas Day,*
*and sent rambunctious people of Treadwell*
*and Douglas and Juneau into the streets*
*to observe the birth of a great nation*
*only thirty-four years past Civil War.*
*Hose races, baseball, and dances ensued*
*through the day; at nightfall Roman candles,*
*sparklers, and pinwheels the children would light*
*to augment the bright fireworks display*
*in the skies high above Treadwell plaza.*
*Into this milieu of celebration*
*bonny Abigail gambled—what she thought—*
*her final chance to win wayward Erik's*
*true heart, now lost to Miss Marie Prideaux.*
*The Highland Sword Dance, the Gillie Challum,*
*she'd perform, ostensibly for the crowds,*
*but really for Erik, and only him.*
*Alas, devious Kearney, on a quest*
*to shadow his quarry—Erik Meyer—*
*discovered the friendship with Abigail*
*and upon reporting this new finding*
*did entangle our heroine anew.*

Glistening fire hoses slithered chaotically behind bouncing hose carts tugged by muscled men in striped shirts.[18] A ragged cluster of European miners—Finns and Germans, Irish and Norwegians, Greeks and Poles, Swedes and a trio of Italians from Rome—pointed and jabbered different languages and laughed as hoses rollicked a few strides beyond their black-booted toes. Next to them, a proud Tlingit Chief, white-man-suit-dressed for the occasion, and his family observed the raucous proceedings with both amusement and ap-

prehension. Countless rambunctious miners, and even a few women and children too, swarmed the rough-edged street along the length of the advancing hoses. High to the south, above the snow-dressed peak of Mount Bradley, warming sunlight glowed between cumulus clouds for the first time in three weeks—a Fourth of July tradition in Treadwell, Alaska.

Erik Meyer bumble-weaved through the Europeans and Tlingit Chief's family searching for Marie and Abigail. He turned abruptly and trotted across the street and hurdled awkwardly over the squirming hoses, nearly tangling his feet when one of the hoses jumped off the muddy ground and slapped his heel.

He searched for Marie because he loved her; he searched for Abigail because he had promised that he would watch her dance at noon, and he always kept his promises—especially with Miss Abigail Sinclair. Kearney followed him through the crowds of unruly miners, about twenty paces back, grinning deviously and chomping a splintered tooth pick. Erik recovered from his near fall then plowed head-long into Abigail, knocking her off her feet. He grabbed her arms—clenched tightly around two Scottish basket-hilt claymore swords—on the way down and yanked her upright, knocking the Glengarry to the ground. "Miss Abigail. I have been on the search for you." Abigail cradled the swords in her right arm and bent down to retrieve the errant hat. "I can see that you have, Mister Erik. And so, now you have found me."

As Abigail rose up from the ground, Erik noticed her delicate black dancing shoes, white-wool-sheathed legs, and bare knees below the clinging hem of the kilt. "Miss Abigail, you are wearing a costume..." and then he blundered into an unintentional remark, "...and it shows your pretty knees." He paused and then looked down. "I am sorry, Miss Abigail. I did not mean to say such a thing."

Abigail feigned distraction from the near fall. "That's alright, Erik. It's a natural mistake to think of this as a costume. It's called a Highland Kilt, and I'm wearing it because of the dance I'm about to perform."[19]

Not knowing any better, Erik breathed deeply with relief that Abigail had not heard his foolish remark. "I have never seen such a thing. It is very pretty. But I did not know that a woman could own swords. Where did you find them in Treadwell? I have not seen such things at the general store."

Kearney had skulked close enough to hear most of the conversation, and noted with profound interest that a close friendship appeared to thrive between Erik and Abigail. He promised himself that he would report this important discovery to Ulrich Boucher before the day's festive conclusion.

Abigail smiled. "I did not find them in Treadwell—I brought them with me from Scotland…in the steamer trunk. You have already carried them many times, Erik."

Erik laughed. "That explains why the trunk is so heavy. I wondered when I lifted it, how it could weigh so much."

"Be thankful then that these are not the ancient claymore broadswords. They would have weighed much more. But then again, they might not have fit in the trunk."

Kearney decided that he had heard enough and vanished beyond the crowd to find Ulrich Boucher. He knew that this new information would please his boss, and possibly lead to a commendation of some sort. He crushed the toothpick vigorously as he imagined the possibilities for advancement.

"Yes, Miss Abigail."

"Are you not wondering, Erik, why I have carried these swords all the way from Scotland?"

"Yes, Miss Abigail."

"They're for the dance I'll be doing today—the Scottish Sword Dance. It's done to the tune of *Gillie Challum*—my father taught me the dance because he had no son to share it with."

"Yes, Miss Abigail."

"I've even found a Scotsman to play the bagpipes for my dance. Did you know that Malcolm McKensie plays the bagpipes, Erik?"

"No, Miss Abigail."

"I heard him practicing a few weeks ago, down by the wharf, when I was taking an evening stroll, and asked him to play for my dance today. Did you hear him practicing, Erik?"

"No, Miss Abigail."

"Do you have nothing to say for yourself then, other than yes and no, Miss Abigail?"

"No…Yes, Miss Abigail."

"Then shall I see you at the dance at noon?"

"Yes, Miss Abigail."

———

A slender man in a black suit, recently-purchased straw boater hat, and dust-streaked black shoes lifted a conical megaphone to the underside of his hawkish nose and shouted at the gathering crowd. "Come all, come all, come all to the front of the grandstands for the performance of an ancient dance never before seen in the history of Treadwell…"

Abigail stood smartly in front of the stands, toes pointed out, heels together, with the claymores crossed on the ground, the hilt of one at her feet, the hilt of the other to her left. A gentle gust of southeast wind rustled the kilt.

"...by our very own Miss Abigail Sinclair, formerly of Edinburgh, a great city of Scotland itself, but now of St. Ann's..."

Abigail set fisted hands on smoothly curving hips, and turned and nodded to Malcolm McKensie. Malcolm breathed breath after breath into the mouthpiece of the blowpipe then slapped the side of the defiant bag to prompt the tenor and bass drones to play the familiar octaves. A dozen children swarmed into a semi-circle beyond the polished swords, their parents, hundreds of miners and other men, and Erik Meyer jostling behind.

"...skillfully accompanied on the authentic Highland Bagpipes by none other than miner extraordinaire Malcolm McKensie, formerly of Glasgow, also a great city of Scotland itself, but now of Treadwell..."

Malcolm began fingering the ancient tune *Gillie Challum* on the chanter. After a few lyric measures, Abigail bowed cleanly at the waist then rose. A glint of sword-blade-reflected sunlight flashed across her face.

"...and now, ladies and gentlemen, directly from the bygone days of Shakespeare's tragic Macbeth, the Scottish Sword Dance!"

Abigail slowly lifted the heel of her right foot and pointed the toe to the side of her left to begin the dance, then in a smooth and unbroken motion skip-hopped deftly to the right of the crossed basket hilt claymore swords and began the dance. As she stepped skillfully around the gleaming blades without ever a touch, sometimes raising both hands charmingly above her head, sometimes lowering them again to her hips, sometimes leaping high above the swords with the kilt swirling across gracefully splayed legs, all in exquisite coordination with the lilting notes of the droning bagpipe, Erik Meyer stood behind the arc of children and their parents and watched in bewildered wonder as an unexpected warmth flowed around his stomach.

———

Ulrich Boucher peered through his second-floor office window across Gastineau Channel to the skies above Treadwell and admired the evening fireworks display. He lifted the window a few inches so that he could hear the explosions of the rockets. A dog barked somewhere down the street. Then he turned again to Kearney and reiterated his question.

"I love the sound of a barking dog in the distant night. You are sure that Meyer and Abigail are close friends then? There is no doubt in your mind?"

Kearney grinned. "I'm sure—no doubt in my mind at all."

"And you are sure that they weren't just exchanging casual conversation in passing?"

"I'm telling you boss, they're about as friendly as two people can get without actually loving each other."

Ulrich slid the window up to its fullest height and, leaning his smooth hands on the freshly-painted window sill, breathed in the evening air, sweet with the fragrant smell of the sea. "Well, then—this does allow a few interesting possibilities."

# Stopes

*Where, I asked, does one enter the mine shaft?*
*A straightforward question, or so I thought.*
*But a simple answer I could not find.*
*Then lo!—I happened upon a photo*
*of the steam-powered Treadwell Hoisting Works,*
*and then a mine layout in Hard Rock Gold,*
*and thereby established the very spot*
*where Erik and the Marino brothers*
*entered Treadwell Mine on that fateful day.*
*Into the cage and down the shaft they plunged,*
*down, down, down, far beneath the day-lit earth*
*to seven-hundred and fifty-foot level—*
*my guess, I confess, of progress that year.*
*And there new stopes advanced—excavations,*
*simply put, formed by drilling and blasting*
*the obstinate rock and ore-bearing veins.*
*And feeling the vibration of a blast,*
*Erik (assured that something was amiss)*
*dropped his shovel of fresh-dug muck and ran*
*to the scene of the blast, and found chaos.*
*Up to here Erik's strength has been mentioned—*
*lifting a steamer trunk, throwing a crate—*
*but now the story explores his true mettle:*
*what lives in spirit and mind beyond strength.*

Thumptrudging by the 240-stamp mill up the narrow steepness of the walk leading to the Treadwell Hoisting Works,[20] Erik Meyer thought of the Scottish Sword Dance and lively *Gillie Challum*. Although two full weeks had passed since the Fourth of July, he could still envision Abigail dancing around the gleaming swords and leaping winsomely high above the ground. The clarity of the vision began to frighten him, but then an empty ore train (returning from the 300-stamp mill to the north and heading up to the hoist works to pick up another load of ore) rattled deafeningly by and purged the disquieting apparition. Erik looked up from the trail in front of his feet, and, for the first time, noticed the stream of miners surrounding him—somehow they had joined him unnoticed.

The Italian twins, Alberto and Paolino Marino, formerly fishermen of Riomaggiore but now miners of Treadwell, tugged on the elbows of Erik's red plaid wool pea coat, Alberto on one sleeve and Paolino on the other. The oldest by nearly three minutes, Alberto spoke first: "Buona sera, Signore Erik. We have followed your striped coat for many minutes now, but you have not listened." Paolino added: "Si, Mister Erik…many minutes, and the coat has not listened."

Erik turned without slowing his pace. "My good friends, the Marino brothers. And how are you two doing this pleasant evening?"

Alberto responded first: "We do nice, Signore Erik. But we did not know you were of the night shift." Paolino added: "No, we did not know you and the night shift."

Erik looked ahead again as he neared the heavy wood-framed iron-hardwared double doors of the hoist works entrance. Steam hissed when the hoist engine slowed to a stop before changing direction. "I work the seven o'clock night shift only this week, then I return to day shift."

Alberto continued the conversation: "That is nice, Signore Erik, for we will have the pleasance of your time for all the week." Paolino added: "Yes, the pleasance of all the week."

Erik reduced his stride as he crossed the threshold into the hoist works and rested his muscular arms around each twin's shoulders. "That is right, my Italian friends. We shall have each other's company for an entire week, but then I must return to day shift and you may not see me in the mine again."

Alberto, with the weight of Erik's strong arm across his neck, replied cheerfully: "This is not a bad thing, Signore Erik. We are sure to spot you at Treadwell Club, and then we can play the billiards." Paolino added "Si, we can play the billiards, and next time we win you."

The iron doors of the cage clanged open and men piled onto the platform. Erik and the Italian twins were the last and the hoist foreman slammed the doors behind them and secured the latch. "We shall see," Erik answered, "but you have not beat me yet."

The hoist engine hissed scalding steam and the cage began an accelerating descent down the shaft of Treadwell mine. As it passed the 220 Foot Level, Paolino spoke first for the first time: "How deep we fall tonight? I do not like the basement."

Erik grinned. "I believe, my good friends, that we are on our way to the 'basement' as you fear." The cage fell past the 330 Foot Level. "There's a stope[21] still to finish there, and that's what we're working on this fine night."

Alberto smelled a momentary whiff of gas as the 440 Foot Level slid by the falling cage. He offered some optimism: "The basement is not so bad—it looks the same as anywhere so can I see."

Paolino gripped the vibrating rail at the edge of the cage as it reached 600 Foot Level. "It could look the same, but I feel it different, so the same it is no."

As the plummeting cage tumbled to the 750 Foot Level and slowed to a stop, Erik finally admitted, "I know what you mean, friend. I know what you mean."

———

Erik set his foot at the back of the shovel blade and drove the tip of the shovel into the shattered ore at the floor of the stope. The man next to him did the same, then they turned and threw the muck[22] into the waiting ore car in unison. Erik stood erectly and rested blister-hardened hands on the wooden shovel handle. The floor shuddered as blasting continued in another stope beyond the shaft. Erik looked down before speaking to the other man.

"Did you feel that?"

The other man bent over and, pressing a dirty finger against the side of his dirty nose, snorted a gob of blackened snot on the floor. "Just another blast somewhere else in the mine. What's to feel?"

"It did not feel right to me. It was too much blast, I think."

"You can feel the difference?"

"I think so. I must go see what has happened." Erik dropped his shovel and ran.

He arrived at a chaotic scene of smothering dust and scattered debris when he reached the entrance to the new 750 Foot Level stope north of the shaft. Two miners limped by, heading for the safety of the shaft. Erik shielded his eyes with one hand and held the other out in front as he plunged into the choking dust. He worked his way along the sidewall of the stope until he found a group of miners with lanterns huddled near the end of a twisted string of overturned ore cars pushed near the side wall of the stope by piles of shattered debris. Erik peered down the row of ore cars. At the end of the narrow passageway, constricted on one side by the inverted ore cars and the other by the jagged side wall of the stope, he spotted an unfortunate miner half-wedged under the mangled coupling between two of the cars. Erik stepped back until he bumped into a man slumped to his knees. He turned and gazed down at a weeping Alberto.

"Alberto, what has happened? Why do you cry?"

Alberto looked up and recognized Erik. "Paolino is caught in the ore cart, and they cannot move him because there is no room for many men."

"What do you mean, no room for many men?"

"There is room only for one man, and it is too much for him."

"To do what? Too much for what?"

"To move the cart above Paolino. There is too much for one man."
Erik understood. "Wait here, Alberto. I will return with your brother."
"But Signore Erik, there is too much—"
"Wait here."
Erik tromped up to the group of miners and grabbed the smallest one by the jacket lapel. "You come with me. When I move the ore car, you pull Paolino behind my legs. You understand?"
The small miner stared at Erik quizzically. "You must be making a joke. No way you're going to move that ore car. We need to clear this muck out so we can get three or four men in there. Take a few hours. No way one man can do it."
Erik pulled the small miner along with him then into the narrow passageway. When they neared within a few feet of Paolino, Erik heard him moan. The path between the upturned ore cars and the stope wall tapered until only Erik could fit next to the end of the car that pinned his friend. Erik reached down and touched Paolino's head and felt a sticky-warm dampness. "We cannot wait to clear the muck. It will take too much time and he will die. When I push against the car, you pull him out—behind my legs like I told you."
The small miner chuckled. "If you can move that damn ore car, I'll gladly pull him to wherever the hell you want."
Erik wedged his back against the side of the car and placed his feet above Paolino's upper body against the base of the opposing wall. His bent his knees and they pressed against an outcrop of blast-sharpened rock. He slid his back down against the rough side of the overturned car until his curled fingers reached the lower edge. With each downward movement the rock tore jagged cuts across his knees.
Erik winced and sucked in three deep breaths. "Ready? I am going to push against the car now."
The small miner did not believe he would have any work to do, and responded casually. "I'm ready as I'll ever be."
Erik grunted deep in his gut and pressed both feet hard against the opposing rock and his back into the side of the car. Veins and arteries surged with fresh blood as his back and legs strained against the impossible load. His heart pumped harder and harder until he could hear the rapidly accelerating beats pounding ominously in his ears. The ligaments of his knees strained until they neared the point of rupture. The corroded iron edge of the car ground into the finger joints of his hands and blood trickled and dripped off his finger-

tips to the floor. And then…the ore car—moved. Erik continued to push against the weight of the car with strength beyond anything he had expected, and the car moved again until Erik's knees began sliding back up and the same blood-stained rocks tore even deeper into his ravaged knees. And when Erik thought that he could bear no more….

"Damn it. I don't believe it! I've got him! I've got him!" The small miner dragged Paolino Marino from beneath the coupling's crushing weight and behind Erik's sweat-lathered-shuddering legs.

Erik held the car for five more seconds, until Paolino was safe, then collapsed.

# Confrontation

*Near daybreak, following the fateful night*
*of Erik's valiant rescue of the twin,*
*Paolino, from beneath the crushing load.*
*Now sitting in the St. Ann's Hospital*
*and awaiting Abigail's tender care,*
*he fabricates a story of untruth*
*to hide the facts of his heroic act.*
*On finding that Erik has two days off*
*Abigail yearns for a little of his time*
*but instead mends and sends him on his way*
*to the waiting charms of Marie Prideaux.*
*Limping to the store and slamming the door,*
*Erik is spied by Ulrich's waiting man—*
*the devious toothpick-munching Kearney—*
*who upon spotting Erik rushes on*
*to do what evil we can only guess.*
*Erik saunters through the general store*
*pretending int'rest in the goods displayed*
*but really there to speak to Miss Marie.*
*Alas, his chat with her is quickly stopped*
*by entrance of the brothers ABC,*
*bearing spite and axe handles hickory.*
*Bold Kearney spews a few misguided threats,*
*and then the test of wills at last begins.*

Abigail listened to the piercing echo of a Varied Thrush drift through the open window of the St. Ann's Hospital in Douglas. Slanting early morning light glowed off the far wall of the small exam room. She studied Erik's bloody knees and tugged a rubber glove over the graceful fingers of her right hand. Erik squirmed when she cleaned around the wounds with soap and water and then bathed the savage lacerations with antiseptic. He jerked when she injected anesthetic cocaine[23] along the edges of the jagged tears.

"Sit still, Erik. You won't last for long when I'm suturing these wounds without a little anesthetic."

Erik held his legs still by pressing down with his hands. "You surprised me, that's all. I can sit as still as you like."

Abigail raised her eyes. "Tell me Erik…how did you manage to hurt yourself so? These wounds are frightful indeed."

Although Abigail had told him to sit still, he squirmed again. "I…I bumped my knees on the wall of the stope. It was a stupid accident. I will not let it happen again."

Abigail's eyes narrowed to doubting slits. "I see. You must have been running full out when you *bumped* your knees on the wall."

Erik liked Abigail's embellishment of his fictional story. "Yes, that is right. I was running…very fast when I hit the wall." Then he added for emphasis, "Very fast."

Abigail threaded catgut through the elongated eye of a curved suture needle then grasped the needle with a forceps. "Then you are very lucky that you did not break your nose as well. Am I correct to assume that you will have a day or two off to rest?" She hoped that this accident, although unfortunate and not to be wished for, might offer a chance for them to spend the evening together.

Erik straightened up and smiled. "Yes, it is true that I will receive a few days off before I must work again. But I am not unhappy with this because it will give me a chance to visit Marie Prideaux at the general store more than once. She is not often there when I finish work, but now I should have no trouble finding her."

Abigail jabbed the suture needle into the edge of the first wound and Erik flinched. "Oh, I'm sorry. I see that the anesthetic has not quite taken effect yet. I was just trying to get you on your way to Marie as quickly as possible, but I'll wait a minute or two."

Erik relaxed into a slouch and exhaled. "Yes, we should wait for a minute. Or maybe two."

Kearney leaned both elbows confidently against a stalled ore car and watched Marie Prideaux walk along the front of the Treadwell General Store before disappearing through the wood-framed entry door. The ore car moved and he stepped away. He swiveled around on one heel and watched the last edge of sun slide behind a shredded band of altocumulus clouds near the southern end of Gastineau Channel. A bald eagle shrieked high above, the sound of the shriek fading into the mountain. When he turned again, Erik Meyer

bounce-limped across the edge of his vision. Kearney's head snapped around just as Erik slammed the door of the general store. Kearney spit his mangled toothpick to the ground, pulled a fresh one out of his unbuttoned shirt pocket, and then trotted away. The purpose of his surveillance had finally arrived, and he had work to do.

Stanislaw Krakowski, born in Chicago of immigrant parents,

stroked his luxurious moustache and, without looking up to see who had entered the store, yelled, "Erik Meyer—do not slam the door when you enter the store."

Erik yanked the newsboy hat off and scrunched it into a lumpy ball. "How did you know it was me?"

"It is always you, Erik. You are the only one in Treadwell who slams the door so."

Erik glanced over at Marie and she looked away. "I am sorry Mister Krakowski, but I always forget."

"Yes, so I have noticed."

Erik sauntered along a table loaded with wood crates inlaid with neat rows of fruit and pretended to study the quality of the day's produce. He looked up and feigned admiration of a huge hanging bunch of bananas, still waiting to ripen, then reached out and squeezed one of the bananas to test its ripeness. As he stepped beyond the end of the fruit-laden table, his eyes bounced along the high shelf below the ceiling loaded with metal cans stacked in the shape of ziggurats and boxes arranged in brick wall running course and other items he could not identify arranged in a manner he could not discern. He veered toward the counter were Stanislaw Krakowski stood behind a wrapping paper dispenser stroking his moustache and eyeing Erik with amusement. When Erik reached the counter, he glided his palm along the wood trim at the edge and slowed his stride. Once he reached within a few paces of Marie he stopped gawkily and looked up with the best expression of surprise he could muster.

"Miss Marie—I did not know you worked in the general store today. You have caught me by much surprise."

Marie Prideaux's charming blue eyes raised up from a wad of packing slips and focused on Erik's mock surprise. "Why, Mister Meyer, how lovely to see you today. And how, might I ask, did you manage a day off from the mine? Unless I am mistaken, I do not believe it is Christmas today."

Erik looked down at his wadded hat. "I had a little trouble at the mine last night, so Mr. Bradley has given me two full days off to get better. I do not work in the mine again until day after tomorrow."

"And what kind of trouble did you have at the mine that merited two full days off?"

"Oh, nothing important. Just a little accident. But I think I am feeling better already."

"An accident? What kind of accident?"

"Just a little one."

"Yes, so you said. And what do you intend to do with your two full—"

The front door to the store swung violently open and slammed against an iron-hooped-wood-staved barrel stuffed with potatoes. Kearney and three stout men stormed in and marched down the center of the store. They stopped behind Erik and formed a ragged semicircle. Kearney grinned past his toothpick and leaned presumptuously against the counter. Two of the men pressed new hickory axe handles against their bulky legs.

"Good morning, Erik. I'd like you to meet three of my new friends, just off the boat from Northern Ireland: Angus, Brogan, and Connell. It's only been a few days, but I've already grown fond of calling them the ABC Brothers—maybe even *you* can figure why."

Erik turned his head just enough to see the munching toothpick, then looked back at Marie. "I have no business with you Kearney, or your new friends the XYZ Boys."

Kearney's grin vanished and he sucked the toothpick into his mouth until only the tip showed. "That's ABC, Erik, and we have business with you, whether you like it or not."

Erik ignored Kearney, and continued his conversation with Marie. "As I was saying, Miss Marie, I have two full days off, and I thought—"

Kearney nodded and Angus grabbed the collar of Erik's red plaid pea coat and yanked him back. Erik's damaged knees throbbed with unexpected pain at the pull and he fell back unable to resist. Kearney flashed a gambler's dagger from his boot and pressed it against Erik's neck. Erik slumped at the touch of the razor-sharp point of the five-inch blade.

"Here's the deal, my powerful but foolish friend. If you speak to Miss Prideaux again, or even look at her in a way me or any of the ABC Brothers here don't like, then it's quite possible that your pretty little nurse friend will get hurt—or maybe worse. You understand?"

Erik stiffened. "If you touch Abigail, I will find you and kill you."

Kearney's grin resumed. "I don't see how you're in any position to threaten me, my helpless friend, but if it makes you feel better—"

Erik's hand shot out and clamped around Kearney's wrist, immobilizing the dagger, then pushed the deadly blade away from his neck with a crushing grip. Kearney squeaked out his next demand. "Let go of my wrist you stupid rube. Let go!"

Brogan raised his new hickory axe handle and slammed Erik across the shoulders, but to his astonishment Erik continued to squeeze Kearney's wrist. Kearney dropped the knife to the floor and whimpered. "Let go of my damn wrist. Let go of my…." Brogan raised the axe handle again, this time gripping it with both hands, and prepared to strike Erik on the top of his head.

Stanislaw Krakowski spoke calmly as he pumped a 12-gauge round into the chamber of his brand new Winchester Model 1897 slide-action shotgun. Brogan froze at the sound. "Erik, better let Mr. Kearney go before you hurt him. And Mr. A or B or C or whichever you are, I think you should put that axe handle away so I don't have to blow your arm off. I wouldn't want to damage that new clothing display right behind you." Erik released Kearney and Brogan dropped the axe handle to the floor with a woody clatter.

Kearney held the crushed wrist with his good hand and hopped around. "You'll pay for this you stupid miner. You'll pay for this. You'll pay."

Stanislaw raised the tenor of his voice, but only slightly. "And I'd advise you to quiet down, Kearney. I wouldn't want to get nervous and accidently blow a hole in you either. Now everyone back away and head out of the store so there's no trouble." Kearney picked up his fallen dagger, shoved it angrily into his boot, and turned to leave the general store. The ABC Brothers followed. Erik prepared to leave as well, but Stanislaw stopped him. "Not you Erik. You can stay if you want."

Marie spoke for the first time since Kearney's blade had thrust against Erik's neck. "Yes, Erik, please stay if you'd like. I'm so sorry this happened. I'm so sorry."

Erik leaned forward against the counter, conscious again of the throbbing pain in his knees. "No need for that, Miss Marie. You have done nothing wrong."

Marie felt her eyes fill with tears. "Oh Erik, but I have done something wrong. I have."

# Rejection

*And now, dear reader, a perilous trip*
*through dark and twisted paths of thought below*
*the conscious mind that swirls on bright-edged sphere*
*of glowing light that forms the haze of self*
*we rashly suppose to compose our truth.*
*Yet which of us foresees the darkest thoughts*
*that wait in hiding ready to ensnare*
*that shining truth with grimly tearing claws*
*to cleave us from anticipated hope*
*until we swim in wretched hopelessness,*
*bewildered by the darkness of true self.*
*But hopelessness is not a certainty,*
*and hope is surely always to be sought*
*when we allow the fundamental truth*
*that we do have choice between the darkness*
*and light that dwell together in our minds.*
*Then who are we to haughtily declare*
*the power of what dwells in thought and mind*
*and why it sways a poor soul to select*
*sad darkness instead of bright-shining light.*
*Should we therefore forgive Ulrich Boucher*
*for choices he has made that emanate*
*from corrupt darkness rather than from light,*
*or should we say a prayer and hope the best?*

Marie stepped with care across the uneven wood-planked board-walk sheathing Front Street in downtown Juneau, her darting eyes seeking the elegantly-clothed figure of Ulrich Boucher. As she walked, heels click-tapping the weathered boards in rapid pace, her delicate dress swirling over slender legs, she considered the words that would clearly express her thoughts and consummate the purpose of the rendezvous. Her mind swarmed with Erik Meyer as well, above all his frightful grasp of Kearney's dagger-wielding hand. She glanced up the street and noticed a group of men gathered in front of the restaurant. As she studied the scene more closely, a surveyor's transit came into view, and a black-suited man holding an oversized sheet of paper. And then she heard the tap-tap-tap of Ulrich's gentleman's umbrella echo from the narrow alley she had just passed. She walked ten more strides before whirling around.

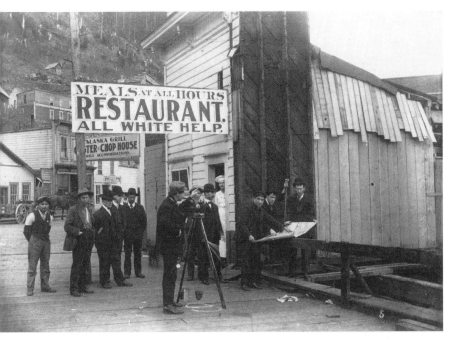

"Mister Boucher—is it your intention to follow me all the way to the restaurant without saying a word?"

Ulrich stopped, tapped the umbrella one last time, then smiled and thrust out a bundle of twelve red roses. "I have brought you fresh flowers to prove the purity of my intentions, Miss Prideaux."

Marie glanced down at the flowers but did not take them. "I have no doubt of the purity of your intentions Ulrich, but we have dinner arrangements, and I would prefer that we avoid further delay."

Ulrich dropped the bouquet to his side, but, surprisingly, smiled more broadly. "As you wish, my decisive dinner date. By all means, we should proceed directly to the restaurant." Then Ulrich spotted the surveying crew and bystanders. "That is, my dear, if we can find a safe path through yonder horde of gawking brutes that blocks our way."

Marie ignored his comment. They walked side-by-side around the gawking horde and into the restaurant without speaking another word.

———

Always the consummate gentleman, Ulrich bowed with a theatric flourish and motioned Marie to her seat at the white-linen-clothed dining table. He bent down as he pushed the chair against her calves and stole a whiff of fragrant hair when she settled into the moving cushion. After quickly seating himself, he snapped his fingers and spoke words drenched with transparent arrogance. "Garçon, garçon—two menus, if you please, and be quick about it." Marie had never heard anyone snap so loudly. She thought to herself that he must have spent many hours in practice.

The waiter, a young man of no more than twenty years and 135 pounds, dressed in clean white shirt and apron, arrived in a few seconds with the menus. He spoke with a fluid mix of respect and fear. "Yes, Mister Boucher. I have your menus right here."

Ulrich flipped his menu open and appeared to study the contents, but selecting an evening meal did not distract him from more serious thoughts. *I must say, that sending Kearney and the ABC Brothers to confront that interfering simpleton with the threat of harm to his Highland wench was indeed a stroke of pure genius. Now that he has no choice but to stay out of the way, the exquisite Marie Prideaux has no choice but to embrace me as her true beau. Yes, Ulrich Boucher, you have outdone yourself this time.*

Marie ordered without looking up from the menu. "I'll take the Waldorf Salad and a glass of white wine. Oh, and please bring some freshly ground pepper as well. Can you do that?"

"Yes, Miss Prideaux, whatever you say." The waiter scribbled some notes on a piece of wrinkled paper then turned to face Ulrich.

*This dinner engagement proves the brilliance of my scheme. Brilliance. Proves it. But who would have imagined that she would have requested it so quickly? The dinner. Who? Absolutely brilliant. Apparently, she can barely wait to ask for my favor. No surprise. No surprise at all. Hardly wait....*

The waiter tapped his pencil on the edge of the table, but heard no response from Ulrich. "Mister Boucher, are you ready to order?"

*Wise to commence the relationship slowly. Wise. Too fast is too much. Too wise is too much. Too much is too much. A few more intimate dinners together, evening walks along the beach, then try a boat trip to Skagway or Sitka. Yes, that would surely woo her heart. To Skagway. Might suggest a private cabin, if all goes well. To Skagway. Yes, that's the ticket. Private cabin to take advantage....*

"Mister Boucher?"

*Then, who knows? Wedding bells in the fall. Big church wedding. She'll want that. I'm sure of it. Appearances important. Children, of course. She'll want that too. Nanny. Must have a nanny to deal with the little brats. Satisfy my lust but must have a nanny. But she can't expect me to remain faithful. Not fair. Too much to ask of a man of my infinite charms. Too much. Too much. Infinite. Charms. Nanny. Must have... a...pretty...nanny. To much to ask of a man. Pretty. Must be....*

Marie finally raised her eyes and closed the menu. "Ulrich, the waiter is waiting to take your order."

*Brilliant plan. ABC and Kearney. Lust, but brats must have a nanny. Highland wench will never know how close she came. How close. Stupid Scottish whore. She could have prevented it, but then. Solved the problem, though. Yes, that's it. Someone pretty. Personally select. Must be someone. Have to look around. Check the goods in Sitka and Skagway. Boat trip. Someone. Marie will never know. Scottish. To take care of the children. She'll want them, but pretty nanny. And then, who knows? Use her up then find another. Nanny? Marie? Damn kids. Never know. Sure of it. Then what?*

Marie reached across the table and touched Ulrich's hand. "Ulrich, the waiter would like to take your order. Have you decided yet?"

Ulrich's eyes snapped up. "Yes, of course. My order. Why yes. I'll have the coq au vin. Now be off with you my good man."

The waiter paused, a chill of fear slithering up his spine. "Uh, Mister Boucher, we don't have any of that. But I can bring you the special if you like?"

Ulrich rolled his eyes in disgust. "Yes, yes, what is the special, then?"

The waiter smiled. "It's the cook's specialty: chicken cooked in red wine."

Ulrich rolled his eyes back. "You must be joking, and yet I see that you are not. Such a pity. Bring me the special, and please use a good wine, not the poison you serve to the indifferent miners who stagger in here. Now off with you. Marie and I have need of privacy."

Ulrich reached across the table and grasped Marie's hand. She pulled it away. "My dear, what is wrong? Has that uncouth serving boy upset you? Please say the word and I will have him disciplined."

Marie frowned. "You'll do no such thing, Ulrich."

"Only a chivalrous offer, my dear. To demonstrate how much I care for you and—"

"Stop, Ulrich. I have something important to say, and I want you to listen."

*More brilliant than I imagined. Now it is. Now! She wants a wedding now, not later. She can't wait. Charms. Not in spring. Then children. Too soon without a nanny. Too. Must move fast to find one. Must move fast to—*

"I have made a terrible mistake, Ulrich. I have failed to clarify my intentions, but now I must make myself perfectly clear before anything more happens that both of us will regret."

*Here's the word! Regrets spurning me at the dance. Regrets talking to Meyer the rube. Has made a terrible mistake. Regrets. Terrible. Meyer! Nanny! Highland wench! Scottish....*

"I must now state clearly..."

*That you are my true love and Meyer the idiot is not and never! I have made a terrible mistake. Terrible. Terrible. Terrible! Highland wench could have prevented so much. Unable to resist my charms. Come to her senses. Finally. Must begin looking for a nanny soon. Must not forget to....*

"...that I believe you are a fundamentally deceitful man, Ulrich, and that it would be best if we do not see each other ever again."

Ulrich's expression of smug arrogance dissolved to stunning blankness. His eyes, for the first time since he had ordered the coq au vin, bored into Marie's with alarming focus. "A deceitful man? You have called me deceitful? Deceitful?"

"I do not intend to hurt your feelings Ulrich, but I must make myself clear before it is too late."

The waiter arrived with the Waldorf Salad and coq au vin on a large oval serving platter. "I rushed your order, Mister Boucher, just like you asked."

Ulrich stood and dropped his crumpled napkin on the table. He paused for three seconds, then slammed his fist beneath the edge of the serving platter. The hapless coq flew across the room and red-splattered against the wall. Marie held her hand to her lips and shuddered. Ulrich quickly regained a calm demeanor. "Deceitful? Too late? My dear, naive Marie…it is already too late."

―――

Kearney fidgeted on the couch as he waited for Ulrich to say something. The grandfather clock across the office reminded him that he had slid into a warm bed only two hours ago before getting the call from an unnaturally calm Ulrich Boucher.

"Kearney—"

"Yes, boss?"

"I want you to take care of Erik Meyer. I want you do it tomorrow night. Do you understand?"

"Yes, I do."

"And I want you to take care of the Scottish nurse as well. Tomorrow night."

"You want us to hurt her?"

"I want you to do whatever you think will get Erik Meyer's attention, assuming he is still around to care."

"Whatever we think?"

Ulrich paused for nearly a minute.

"Boss, you said whatever we think?"

"I've changed my mind. You and the ABC Brothers take care of Erik Meyer. I shall deal with the lovely Miss Abigail Sinclair—personally."

*Segue*

# Vengeance

## SCENE ONE

*The next night, 11:04 pm. Remarkable for Juneau,
the ashen skies above the northern Chilkat Mountains
pulse with flashes of light, and the muted echo of
thunder rattles along the sides Gastineau Channel.
A scent of rain imbues the cooling air with foreboding.
Erik Meyer leaves the Windsor Saloon after a few
beers with two friends and strides along Second Street.
Kearney and the ABC Brothers have been waiting in
an alley across from the saloon for nearly two hours.
They follow Erik, staying thirty paces back. Erik turns
at Gold Street and walks up the hill. Kearney and the
Brothers quicken their pace until they follow within
thirty feet. When he reaches Third Street, Erik pivots
east and walks along a narrow boardwalk until he
reaches a secluded opening between two houses. Kearney
and the ABC Brothers break into a jog. Erik hears the
approaching footfalls on the creaking boards and swings
around. His pursuers slow to a casual stroll as they approach
Erik then stop in front of him, only a few feet away.
Kearney is empty handed, but Angus, Brogan, and
Connell each grip a new hickory axe handle in their
grimy hands. Connell slaps the axe handle against his
leg and grins. Angus and Brogan do not move. The dark
clouds behind Kearney and the Brothers light up—a
dull crackle of sound arrives a few seconds later.*

ERIK (*glancing up at the flash of light*): What is this then, Kearney? Why do you and your friends follow me late at night?

KEARNEY (*munching on his fifth toothpick of the day, he removes it before speaking*): Just here to follow Mr. Boucher's orders. That's all, Erik.

ERIK (*suspicious, but smiling*): And what is it your boss has asked you to do at this time of night? Are you on a search for your lost axe heads?

CONNELL (*sniffing back a string of snot*): Can I whack him now? This one has a big mouth and—

KEARNEY (*his voice crackling with anger*): Shut up Connell. Let

me do the talking. Very funny, Erik, but then, you always was the amusing type.

ERIK (*the smile gone*): If that is all you have to say, then I will be on my way. I must get some sleep before work, and I do not have time for this silly talk.

KEARNEY (*stepping back*): Alright, Erik. I can appreciate a man who does not want his time wasted. So here it is. I have two orders from the boss. The first is to deliver a message.

ERIK (*leaning a bit*): A message?

CONNELL (*slapping the axe handle on his leg*): Yeah, a message. KEARNEY (*without turning*): Connell. I told you to shut the hell up. Okay Erik, here it is. Seems you didn't do a good enough job separating yourself from the Prideaux woman, so now your nurse friend is going to get hurt.

ERIK (*his hands clenching, steps toward Kearney and pauses*): You… you would threaten to hurt my Abigail? I would never let you do that. You will not leave here to hurt her. I will stop you!

KEARNEY (*shoves the toothpick back in his mouth and laughs*): That's a good one, Erik. But you've got a small problem my thoughtless friend. I'm not going to hurt her. Ulrich Boucher is going to take care of it himself. As a matter of fact, he should arrive there in a short while, so there's nothing you can do to stop it. I don't think she'll look so good to you after he finishes with her tonight. Hell, she may not even be able to—

ERIK (*takes a step, but Connell jabs the end of the axe handle into his chest*): Out of my way alphabet boy. I will not let anyone hurt Abigail.

KEARNEY (*taking a step behind Connell*): And that brings us to the second order, Erik—to hurt you too, so you can forget about rescuing your little Highland sweetheart. She's doomed, and there's nothing you can do to save her.

CONNELL (*pushing the axe handle harder*): Yeah, nothing you can do about it.

KEARNEY (*turns toward Connell*): For the last time, Connell, I told you to shut—

ERIK (*with tremendous speed and strength, snatches the axe handle from Connell's hand and breaks it in two over his raised leg*): If you do not step out of my way, I will kill you. I will not let your boss hurt Abigail. I will not.

KEARNEY (*stepping back again*): That's enough. Take him out, boys.

*Angus and Brogan raise their axe handles to strike Erik. Erik glares at Kearney, and does not appear to see the approaching attack. Then, just as the two axe handles begin their descent, Erik's right and left hands, still gripping the splintered hickory, explode apart and smash each man on the ear with a ferocity that drives both down writhing to the ground. Connell begins to reach into his jacket, but Erik swings the hickory clubs up and slams them down on Connell's shoulders with frightful impact. Connell crumbles to the ground, waves of pain rolling down his arms and across his chest.*

ERIK (*drops the hickory clubs to the ground and pushes past the astonished Kearney*): Out of my way, little man. This Ulrich Boucher will not hurt Abigail. I will die before I let him.

KEARNEY (*reaching into his jacket as he watches Erik break into a run*): Then that's just what you'll do, you pathetic fool.

*Kearney pulls a Colt Model 1892 .38 Caliber Revolver from his jacket, aims at Erik's receding back, and fires. The bullet misses above Erik's head. Erik turns to look back then increases his pace. Kearney takes more careful aim for his second shot. He squeezes the trigger and the revolver kicks. The bullet strikes Erik in the leg, just below the hem of his pea coat. Erik takes five more steps, his foot dragging at the end, then collapses to the boardwalk. Kearney shoves the pistol into his jacket, picks up Brogan's errant hickory axe handle, and strolls toward Erik.*

ERIK (*pushing himself up and raising his arm*): My Abigail. My dearest Abigail.

KEARNEY (*now standing above Erik, raises the hickory axe handle*): Not anymore, you stupid miner.

ERIK (*as the axe handle strikes the back of his neck with vengeful force*): Abigail, I love y—

KEARNEY (*takes a watch out of his pocket and studies the dial*): Hmmm. 11:19. Not bad. Still time to get a drink and some sleep before I meet Ulrich back at the office.

## SCENE TWO

*Abigail's quarters. 11:01 pm. Abigail has changed into a cotton nightgown and is writing in her diary at a simple wooden desk next to the window. A kerosene lamp provides the room's only light. Smokey is curled into a classic cat pose on the bed next to the desk. The canvas-covered steamer trunk is open at the foot of the bed. A cup of freshly-brewed tea steams a few inches beyond the diary. Abigail writes a few words then lifts the cup and sips the tea. Thunder rumbles to the north, but there is no sound of rain on the roof. As Abigail sets the cup of tea back on the waiting saucer, three staccato taps resonate on the door. Smokey raises his head and meows. Abigail stands and walks to the door. She pauses. Three more taps sound on the door. She opens the door and peers through the crack.*

ABIGAIL (*recognizing Ulrich*): Mister Boucher. What a surprise to find you at my door at this time of night. I was just about to retire.

ULRICH (*tipping his head slightly, his voice calmly suave*): Good evening, Miss Sinclair. May I step into your quaint abode? I fear that it may rain any moment, and I have business with you.

ABIGAIL (*suspicious, but not certain why*): I do not think that would be appropriate, sir. I have changed into my night clothes and am not prepared to receive visitors. I'm sure the business can wait until tomorrow.

ULRICH (*pushes the door open and steps in*) But my dear, that is where you are sorely mistaken. The business cannot wait.

ABIGAIL (*backs away from Ulrich until she bumps the edge of the canvas-covered steamer trunk*): Mister Boucher! This behavior is not appropriate. I demand that you leave at once.

ULRICH (*smiling elegantly and lifting the umbrella until he grips it in both hands*): I wish it were that simple my dear, but alas, I must complete this unfortunate business before midnight, and there is no way to stop it now. Your imprudent friend, Erik Meyer, has seen to that.

*With a gallant flourish, Ulrich slides the rapier fencing blade from the umbrella scabbard and whips it through the air with a lightning flick of his wrist. Distant thunder echoes across the channel as the rapier comes to rest. The light of the kerosene lamp glints on the polished blade.*

ABIGAIL (*her hand fumbling behind her back in the steamer trunk*): What is the meaning of this, Mister Boucher?

ULRICH (*taking a step toward Abigail and brandishing the weapon aggressively*): What is the meaning? How sweet of you to ask, my unfortunate Highland wench. It is simple my dear. I am here to inflict vengeance upon the rube Erik Meyer. Nothing more, nothing less.

*Abigail's hand finds the hilt of one of the claymore swords. She lifts the sword from the canvas covered trunk and unsheathes the lethal blade by whipping the sword across her body. The scabbard flies across the room and slaps against the wall.*

ABIGAIL (*holding the claymore out, the tip aimed at Ulrich's heart*): What have you done to Erik, you pathetic rogue?

ULRICH (*impressed by the sight of the claymore*): My, my, my…what

75

have we here? And I imagined this a boring task. Now am I to be tested by a Valkyrie?

ABIGAIL (*her voice hardening*): Odin's handmaiden I am not, Mister Boucher, but it will please me to send your soul to Valhalla nonetheless.

ULRICH (*moving to attack*): Then I shall enjoy carving you up, Miss Abigail, so much the more.

*Ulrich takes two quick steps and thrusts the blade at Abigail's leg. Abigail steps deftly aside and parries the thrust. Ulrich quickly swings the razor-sharp tip of the rapier across Abigail's other leg, but she skips back and parries again. Ulrich steps back as well, and holds his blade at the ready for the next attack.*

ULRICH: You have skill with the sword, Miss Abigail. I must admit that I am duly impressed.

ABIGAIL (*her voice slightly nervous now*): My father taught me more than to dance with the swords. I will not let you take me easily.

ULRICH (*almost smirking with arrogance*): That he may have done, but I have trained with the finest swordsmen of Europe, my sweet. I am afraid that you will soon find yourself sorely out-matched.

ABIGAIL (*her voice regaining a saucy tone*): Then do you worst sir, and we shall see.

*Ulrich moves left. Abigail slowly turns to follow him. He feints a thrust to his left. She moves to block, then, with lightning speed, he spins around and slashes the sharpened tip of the rapier across Abigail's left thigh. Blood spreads across the cleanly sliced edges of the torn nightgown. Abigail soughs.*

ULRICH (*now enjoying himself*): You are good, Miss Abigail, but not good enough to save yourself tonight. This is just the beginning, my dear.

ABIGAIL (*growing more defiant*): You may have the skill, Mister Boucher, but I have the heart, and will resist you with all of it.

ULRICH (*laughs derisively*): Then maybe, my sweet darling, we should end this silly duel and complete the business at hand. En garde!

*Ulrich salutes Abigail, then resumes the attack. She parries three more thrusts before he slashes the razor tip across her other leg at exactly the same height. Abigail, both thighs cut, blood dripping down her legs to the wooden floor, can no longer move with sufficient speed to defend herself. Ulrich steps back to fully appreciate her helplessness.*

ULRICH (*gleaming with pride at his handiwork*): I fear, Miss Sinclair, that I have ruined your lovely nightgown. I would offer to buy you a new one, but after tonight, I do not think you will have the need.

ABIGAIL (*defiant to the end*): I am not finished yet, butcher. And now it is my turn to say en garde!

ULRICH (*yawning*): I tire of this play. It is time to disarm you and complete my business so that I can be on my way.

*Ulrich feints slowly to the left, then quickly to the right, then with dazzling speed lunges to the left again. Abigail does not move quickly enough to parry the surprise attack, and Ulrich's deadly blade stabs cleanly through Abigail's sword arm just below the shoulder. Her arm falls limply to her side, but she does not drop the claymore.*

ULRICH (*now standing casually and admiring the blooded rapier blade*): I'm afraid the game is over, sweet Abigail. Now I must finish my business, and you will not be able to resist. Such a pity.

ABIGAIL (*soughing*): You are a cruel scoundrel, Ulrich. I pray that someone sends you to hell!

ULRICH (*smiling and leaning forward*): Pray all you want, Abigail. It will do you no good. I think that I shall carve your lovely bosom first, before I move to your pretty face. Goodbye, my dear, goodbye.

*As Ulrich steps forward and raises his blade, Smokey, eager to join the game, rushes from beneath the bed and claws at Ulrich's ankle.*

ULRICH (*surprised, looks down and then kicks Smokey in the side*): Begone horrid beast. I do not have time to play with you. I have more important business at the moment.

*As Ulrich chides the cat, Abigail reaches her left arm across her body and takes the hilt of the claymore in her left hand. She raises the sword with her remaining strength, and, with pain ravaging her legs, lunges forward and thrusts the blade cleanly through Ulrich's chest. She releases the shuddering hilt and falls back against the wall.*

ULRICH (*incredulous and speaking with difficulty*): Oh foul luck, what is this? How? I crippled your arm. Crippled it! How…could you?

ABIGAIL (*panting and holding her wounded arm*): I am ambidextrous, Mister Boucher, and my father taught me to use the claymore with both hands. Your arrogance has killed you.

ULRICH (*slumping to his knees, blood gurgling in his throat and bubbling around his lips as he speaks*): Foul luck. Foul luck! Defeated by a… Highland wench. Oh foul, foul…luck! Defeated by…a…Scottish—

ABIGAIL (*speaking as Ulrich falls to the floor, impaling himself on the claymore blade to the hilt*): Poor lost soul. I did not expect that my prayer would be answered so promptly.

## SCENE THREE

*Early the next morning, 12:47 am. The intersection of Third and Gold Streets. Alberto and Paolino Marino have left the Windsor Saloon and are walking to the house where they are staying until Paolino fully recovers from his broken leg. Both are drunk, and Paolino is finding it difficult to walk with crutches in this condition. A light rain has begun, and the boardwalk streets glisten with fresh moisture.*

ALBERTO (*his speech slurred with alcohol*): I told you not to take so much drink. I am troubled walking, and I do not do it with the crutches as you.

PAOLINO (*burps before responding*): You worry too much of me, my large brother. I will do the crutches fine. You must worry of you before you fall.

ALBERTO (*spotting a dark shape ahead*): And what do we think that is, my drunken brother? Another man has too much of the drink, and now sleeps in the road. Should we wake him before the rain fills him up too much?

PAOLINO (*pensive*): I think we should. It would not do right to leave him in the rain.

*The Marino brothers stagger ahead and finally reach the man. They stand there, both looking down, for nearly a minute before Paolino recognizes Erik Meyer. The realization snaps him from his state of inebriation.*

PAOLINO (*dropping his crutches and falling to the ground next to Erik*): Holiest ships, my brother. It is our true friend Erik Meyer. But why does he sit here in the road in the rain?

ALBERTO (*shocked, slumps to his knees too*): It *is* Erik, but someone has robbed his coat, and he has only the shirt for the rain.

PAOLINO (*agitated*): We must find the help. He is too much for us to carry. I will stay here. You run to get the help.

ALBERTO (*standing and looking around*): I will run, but where should I go?

PAOLINO (*thoughtful*): Find Miss Abigail. She will know what to do.

ALBERTO (*brightening*): Yes, that is good. I will run and find Miss Abigail.

PAOLINO (*more worried now*): Then run, my brother. Run! Find the help soon. Run! Run!

# Comedy

*Poor arrogant Ulrich Boucher is dead,*
*and sucked into the vacuum of his loss*
*the remains of his brutal gang must fall.*
*And now, my friend, a well-deserved reprieve*
*from darkness and the villain's wicked mind*
*to observe the other side of the coin,*
*as it were, and maybe enjoy a laugh*
*before this story's closing chapters end.*
*But then again, laughter you may not gain*
*because the narrow path from tragedy*
*to comedy is sometimes hard to find*
*and fraught with perception's anomalies.*
*So push on, and see if humor you earn*
*and a laugh (or two) as you read the words.*
*Yet, what if you read to the very end*
*without the faintest glimmer of a smile?*
*Should you worry that a sense of humor*
*you do not have? (a tragic conclusion)*
*But then again—after reading the words*
*that follow this introductory poem—*
*what if you laugh so hard that people look*
*to see what mischief lurks beyond their sight?*
*God help us! There are no simple answers.*
*I recommend you worry either way.*

*Ulrich Boucher's office in Juneau, 8:57 am*

Kearney rested a pair of mud-splattered boots on the hand-carved edge of Ulrich Boucher's mahogany pedestal desk and leaned back in the companion leather-cushioned banker's chair. He twirled one of Ulrich's imported Cuban cigars in one hand and worked a toothpick in the other. The ABC Brothers and four other men stood in front of the desk, waiting for Kearney to give them instructions. After spinning the cigar a few more times, Kearney yanked the toothpick and began snare drum tapping the imported cigar on his leg.

"Well, boys, I surely don't know what's happened to the boss. He told me to meet him here at seven sharp, and I can't remember the last time he missed an appointment."

Connell fidgeted. "Maybe you got the wrong time or something."

Kearney sneered. "Don't talk, Connell. Just don't say anything. I didn't get the wrong time. But no matter whether I did or not. The boss gave me a job to do and I'm going to do it, so listen carefully." Kearney slid his boots off the desk and stood, then strolled to the window and peered at the rain. "The boss found out that F.W. Bradley has started some sort of experimental operation at the Treadwell machine shop to manufacture dynamite so he doesn't have to ship it in all the time.[24] Supposed to save money, or something. I want the ABC Brothers to go there tonight and procure some of it. Might come in handy for some plans we got in mind for next week. The rest of you stay here—I've got a special assignment for you. You all understand?"

The ABC Brothers and the four men all nodded, then Connell asked, "What time tonight?"

Kearney paused in disgust. "When do you think? When no one's around, that's when. Dinner time might be a good choice. Think you can handle that?"

Without thinking, Connell offered Kearney a new title. "Yes, boss. We can handle that."

"And Connell—"

"Yes, boss?"

"Why in hell are you wearing Erik Meyer's red plaid jacket? Get rid of it before someone figures out what's going on."

"It's spoils, boss."

"Get rid of it."

———

*St. Ann's Hospital in Juneau, 10:34 am*

Half-asleep, Alberto and Paolino Marino slumped in hard wooden chairs next to Erik Meyer's motionless body. Abigail adjusted her arm sling then leaned on the curved handle of the wooden cane Dr. Molony had shoved into her hand after finishing the last stitch above her left knee.

Dr. Molony bent over the bed and lifted one of Erik's eyelids. "Can't tell when he'll come to. Hard to guess. I'm sorry to say there's a chance he may never wake up."

Abigail thought of Ulrich Boucher and squeezed the handle of the cane. "He's a strong one, so his chances are good. We'll just have to wait. But in the meantime, we mustn't let anyone know he is here at the hospital. Whoever did this might want to find him again and finish the job."

Dr. Molony looked up at Abigail. "And they might want to find you as well to, as you say, finish the job."

Abigail's hand relaxed on the cane. "I'm more worried about Erik. I think the only one who might come looking for me is already dead."

"Maybe so, but I think it wise to keep your presence here a secret too, at least until the marshal sorts this awful mess out."

"I'm not planning on going anywhere doctor, at least until I know Erik is safe."

Dr. Molony glanced over at the Italian twins. Alberto had begun snoring and Paolino rested his head against Alberto's chest. "I don't think you have to worry about anything with these two on guard."

Abigail smiled. "Guard's they may not be, but they saved Erik's life, and for that, Dr. Molony, I shall remain forever thankful."

---

*Ulrich Boucher's office in Juneau, 4:07 pm*

Kearney leaned back in the banker's chair and puffed heartily on his third Cuban cigar of the day, sucking with relish and exhaling cascading plumes of billowing blue smoke. The four men had returned from Kearney's special assignment and had just finished reporting their findings.

"Let me get this straight. You're telling me that he was impaled clear up to the hilt? On a damned broad sword? You're sure about this? It just doesn't make any sense."

The man on the left spoke first. "Pretty hard to miss, boss. Saw the whole thing clearly when the marshal and two deputies carried him out of the house. He was still wearing the sword."

"And you're absolutely sure it was Ulrich? Absolutely sure?"

The second man on the left answered next. "We're sure. That was Ulrich stuck on that sword alright. Bet it hurt like hell when it went in."

Kearney covered his smile with the cigar. "No doubt. But he couldn't have lasted very long, stuck on a sword like that."

The third man spoke next. "No doubt."

Kearney stood. "Well, this does put a new twist on things. I suppose I'm in charge of the gang now, seeing how that was Ulrich's last wish."

The fourth man finally spoke. "No doubt."

Kearney continued. "We should all go to the funeral, of course, so there's at least a few people there. But before that, I think I'll arrange this office more to my liking. The four of you can stay and help me move the furniture."

---

*Treadwell Machine Shop, 6:37 pm*

Angus pushed himself up and sneaked a quick look above the window sill at the north end of the machine shop. Brogan and Connell huddled nearby, maintaining a keen lookout.

Brogan, usually the quiet one, sniffed then asked, "I thought Kearney told you to get rid of that jacket, Connell? How come you're still wearing it?"

Connell pulled the jacket collar around his neck. "It's spoils, brother. I'm going to wear it just for the day. I'll get rid of it tomorrow. I promise I will."

Angus slid back down and crouched on his haunches. "Looks all clear to me. Everyone must be at dinner—just like Kearney said."

Brogan sniffed again. "Okay, then. Let's go."

The ABC Brothers shambled along the side of the machine shop, all six hands touching the rough siding of the building, until they found an entry door. Angus, in the lead, stopped abruptly and Brogan and Connell bumped into him.

Angus reached out to turn the door knob then froze. "Maybe I should just kick it in. We're supposed to be breaking in, after all."

Connell scratched his head. "I think you're right, brother. Why don't all three of us kick it in."

Brogan lined himself up. "Then let's do it."

Angus stood to Brogan's right, and Connell to his left, and the ABC Brothers lunged and kicked at the door in unison. The three plunged headlong into the machine shop in a tangled crash as the door flew open with unexpected ease.

Brogan spoke first. "I don't think the damn thing was latched."

Connell responded, "I think you're right. We should just try the knob next time."

---

*Superintendent's House in Treadwell, 6:40 pm*

Balancing a cup of tea in one hand and a crisp copy of the *Daily Alaska Dispatch*[25] newspaper in the other, F.W. Bradley retired to his study after a hearty dinner of roast beef, boiled potatoes, and fresh bread. He walked across the hardwood floor, nearly catching his toe on a throw rug, and settled into his beloved Shaker rocking chair, taking care not to spill the tea. He set the tea down on a side table and folded the newspaper across his legs, then closed his eyes for a minute and listened to the rain as he rocked. He noted to himself that the intensity of the rain had picked up a little since dinner.

---

*Treadwell Machine Shop, 6:51 pm*

Connell stood at the far north end of the machine shop and admired the bag of golf clubs he had found leaned up against a sturdy sawhorse. He pulled a heavy driver from the bag and whipped it back and forth. "Hey brothers, come and look at these golf clubs. It's quite a set. What do ya suppose they're doing here in the shop?"

Angus answered with an annoyed tone. "Who cares what they're doing here. We're not looking for golf clubs, Connell. We're looking for the dynamite, remember?"

Brogan yelled with excitement. "I think I've found something boys. Come take a look."

The three brothers gathered around a large metal box at the end of a wood work table cluttered with strange glass and steel implements. Someone had screwed a sign with red letters to the front of the box.

Connell squirmed his face as he stared at the sign. "I can't make it out. Brogan, you're good with the letters. What does it say?"

Brogan squinted as he mouthed each letter. "The letters say D...A...N...G...E...R...N...I...T...R...O."

Connell brightened. "This may be exactly what we're looking for. Open her up and let's take a look inside."

Angus turned the handle and opened the door. Water dripped out from the bottom of the box. "What's this about? It's full of ice." He stuck his hand into the box and fished around. After a few seconds, he pulled out a small porcelain sphere with a tiny neck sealed with a cork. "And what do you suppose this is?"

Connell grabbed the white-glazed sphere from Angus's outstretched hand and tossed it in the air five times, nearly dropping it twice. "It's not dynamite, that's for sure, but it'll make a fine golf ball, and that's for sure too. I've been dying to give this driver a try, and now's my chance." Connell set the sphere on the floor and carefully balanced it upside-down on the cork stopper. "Stand back boys, so I have plenty of room to take a good swing. Let's see if I can hit this all the way to the other end of the machine shop."[26]

Angus and Brogan stepped back a few paces. Connell set his feet firmly and wiggled the driver head back and forth a few times before setting the face neatly behind the porcelain sphere. "I used to play a pretty good game of golf in my time. Let's see if I can still bang one down the fairway like I used to." Connell swung the club back until it paused briefly above his head, then whipped it forward in a sweeping arc with a lightning snap of his wrists and at the same instant he shifted his weight and rotated his hips to maximize the power of impact and—

*Superintendent's House in Treadwell, 7:04 pm*

Superintendent F.W. Bradley heard the boom of thunder and a second later the tea cup rattled on the saucer. He looked out the window for lightning but instead noticed black smoke spewing from the north end of the machine shop. The *Daily Alaska Dispatch* trailed in fluttered disarray as he ran from the study.

*Treadwell Machine Shop, 7:10 pm*

F.W. Bradley arrived at the north end of the machine shop a few minutes before the Treadwell Fire Department pulled up. There wasn't much fire—mostly a lot of smoke. Twenty minutes later the firefighters had sufficiently doused everything to remove any danger to the rest of the shop.

A soot-blackened man walked up to F.W. Bradley holding a wad of something in his hand. "Mr. Bradley, I thought you might find this interesting."

F.W. Bradley looked down at the wad and then poked at it with two fingers. "What is it?"

"I could be wrong, but it looks like a chunk of Erik Meyer's red plaid jacket to me. If you look close you can see the red stripes."

F.W. Bradley studied the wad closer and poked it again. "My goodness, I think you're right. But what was Erik Meyer doing in the machine shop at this time of night?"

The soot-blackened man stuffed the wad under his arm. "Haven't a clue. But we'll never find out now. This is all that's left of him."

# News

Newspapers abound in early Juneau,
and nearby Douglas and Treadwell of course.
The Alaska Free Press, earliest known,
beginning in eighteen-eighty-seven
and ending its run a mere four years hence.
Next the Juneau City Mining Record
flourished from the year eighteen-eighty-eight
to four years after the decade began.
Many others commenced in quick order:
the Alaska Journal in ninety-three;
Alaska News in the very same year;
Alaska Mining Record—ninety-four;
the Douglas Miner two years after that;
the Fort Wrangell News began ninety-eight;
and the year of our story (ninety-nine)
five newspapers circulated at once.
In no particular order or rank,
the names of the five newspapers are thus:
the Alaska Truth (truly a grand hope!);
the Sunday Sun (I assume once a week);
Daily Alaska Dispatch (every day);
Daily Alaska Miner (pertinent);
and last, the Daily Evening Record
and Weekly Mining Report (took two lines).

Abigail Sinclair had slept fitfully through the night wedged into a hard wooden chair next to Erik's hospital bed. Dr. Molony let her sleep until 10:55 am before waking her by gently nudging her good arm. Abigail sat up stiffly in the chair, yawned tom boyishly without covering her mouth, and peered through the window. The rain had stopped and she could see blue skies to the south. "What time is it? Did Erik wake up?"

Dr. Molony waved a rolled-up copy of the *Daily Alaska Dispatch* in front of his face as he spoke. He balanced a cup of coffee for Abigail in his free hand. "Nearly eleven. And no, he hasn't come around yet.

But that's not why I woke you. I thought you should know that, according to the paper, Erik must have gone out sleepwalking last night. Would you like a fresh cup of coffee? I made it myself."

Abigail snatched the newspaper from Dr. Molony's hand and quickly unrolled it; he nearly dropped the cup of coffee. She scanned the front page. A large photo of the north end of the Treadwell Machine Shop shrouded in smoke was accompanied by the following headline and story:

## EXPLOSION ROCKS SHOP
### Last night, just a few minutes after 7:00 pm, a mysterious explosion emanated from the north

end of the Treadwell Machine Shop. Superintendent F.W. Bradley and the Treadwell Fire Department were on the scene within minutes. Under Mr. Bradley's expert leadership, the fire was extinguished within minutes. Firefighters sifting through the debris found few clues to explain what had happened. However, there is irrefutable evidence that one Erik Meyer, a miner of Treadwell, was killed in the explosion. Superintendent Bradley promised that he would launch a full....

Abigail scrunched her face as she folded the paper on her lap and smoothed the creases with the palm of her hand. "I'd like that cup of coffee now. How could anyone think that Erik was involved in this? It isn't even possible."

Dr. Molony lowered the saucer and cup of steaming coffee into Abigail's sling-supported hand. "Well, dear, you know the papers. Can't trust everything they say, I suppose."

Abigail lifted the cup to her mouth and sipped. "That may be true, Dr. Molony, but this is an egregious error by anyone's standard."

Dr. Molony smiled, but did not say anything.

———

Stanislaw Krakowski followed the motion of Marie Prideaux's hands as she stacked a new pyramid of cans on the other side of the Treadwell General Store, then returned his eyes to the front page of the *Daily Alaska Dispatch*. He reviewed the photograph again before reading the fifth sentence a third time: *Erik Meyer...was killed...was killed...was killed....* Marie dropped one of the cans and he looked up. The can rolled along the floor unevenly.

"Marie, could you please come over here?"

Marie bent at the knees to retrieve the can. "I'm sorry about the can, Mr. Krakowski. It just slipped out of my hand. I don't think it is damaged."

"I don't care about the can, Marie. Don't worry about it. I just need to talk to you about something important."

Marie set the can on a table display of work clothes as she walked by, then crossed the store until she stood on the other side of the counter from Stanislaw Krakowski. "What is it?"

Stanislaw paused for a full seven seconds. "It's always hard to give someone news like this, so I'll just go right out and say it plain. Erik Meyer is...he's dead, my dear. Killed last night...in an explosion."

Marie sucked in an impulsive breath and covered her mouth with both hands. "Killed. How? Where?"

Stanislaw raised the paper and pretended to read so that he didn't have to look at Marie's eyes. "Around seven, according to the paper. An explosion, as I said. Treadwell Machine Shop. They don't know how it happened, but Erik was killed in the explosion. They're sure of it. That's all it says."

Tears streamed down Marie's cheeks. "Erik, dead? Dead? Killed in an explosion. Oh my God!"

"I'm sorry my dear. I truly am."

Marie began crying in earnest. "I don't believe it. How can this be true? How can it?"

Stanislaw ruffled the paper for effect. "The paper says irrefutable evidence. He's gone Marie. Gone."

Marie concealed her tears with trembling hands. "Oh, Mr. Krakowski. I've made such a mess of things. Such a mess..."

"It's not your fault, Marie. Probably some sort of accident. Not your fault."

Oh, but it is my fault, Mr. Krakowski. It is."

—— ——

Kearney studied the black and white photo of the smoldering machine shop on the front page of the *Daily Alaska Dispatch* with a perverted blend of disgust and amusement. "Those imbeciles! I send them to do a simple job and instead they blow the damn place up. And themselves to boot."

One of the remaining members of his gang shuffled in front of the recently relocated mahogany pedestal desk and spoke with caution. "At least the paper thinks someone else did it."

Kearney wadded the *Daily Alaska Dispatch* into a ball and threw it across the office. Then, almost casually, he intertwined the fingers of both hands neatly on his lap and leaned back in the chair. "You have a point there. You do have a point. The paper thinks the rube Erik Meyer caused the explosion. And if that's the case, so does the marshal. I guess that is the proverbial silver lining to an otherwise dark cloud."

"Guess so."

"But what I want to know…"

"What's that?"

"…is how he managed to get himself over to the machine shop in Treadwell with a bullet in his leg and a lump the size of a golf ball on the back of his head."

"He's pretty strong. I've heard stories."

"You mean that foolish fairy tale about him lifting the ore car off one of the Marino brothers? That story's a pile of crap. No way that could have happened. No way at all."

"I don't know. He's pretty strong."

"No one's that strong. No one. Not even the legendary Erik Meyer." The man shuffled again. "Then what about that nurse. What do you want to do about her?"

Kearney pushed himself out of the chair and walked over to the window—a habit he had learned from Ulrich Boucher. "Abigail Sinclair? Yes, that is a question." Kearney rested a hand on the window sill and looked down at the board-sheathed street.

After waiting a long time for a response, the man interrupted Kearney's reverie. "You want us to finish the job?"

Kearney turned and looked straight into the man's eyes. "Finish the job?" Kearney paused again.

"Yeah. You want us to finish it?"

Kearney returned his gaze to the window. "My dear fellow. Abigail Sinclair was Ulrich's obsession, not mine. Frankly, I rather admire the lady, and see no point. No. Let her be. I don't want anyone harming a hair on her head. You understand?"

"Yes sir."

"Not a hair."

"I got it. Not a hair."

———

Stanislaw Krakowski and Marie Prideaux embraced in a hug of condolence next to the wrapping paper dispenser. Marie pressed her face into the tweedy shoulder of Stanislaw's coat and sniffled.

Stanislaw gently pushed Marie away and spoke in sympathetic tones. "What will you do now, my dear, now that Erik's gone?"

Marie wiped her eyes with the sleeve of her blouse. "I think I shall leave, Stanislaw. I cannot stay here any longer."

Stanislaw nodded. "I understand, and I think that's a good idea. You should take a day off and get some rest. You'll feel better after that."

"No, Stanislaw. You do not understand. I mean that I shall leave Treadwell."

"You mean, leave town, for good?"

"Yes, for good. There is nothing left for me here but memories of death and tragedy. I shall pack my things and depart tomorrow morning on the southbound steamer."

"Tomorrow? But what will you do?"

"It does not matter. I simply must leave before I am overcome by the misery of this place."

Stanislaw Krakowski could not think of anything more to say, so he hugged Marie one last time. But now she stood limply in his embrace, her tear-damp hands hanging lifelessly by her sides.

# Departure

And now, my friend, we have come to the end
of the story of Abigail Sinclair,
bonnie heroine of my writer's mind;
and Erik Meyer of mythic resolve;
of Ulrich Boucher who played his role well;
and Marie Prideaux, who could forget her;
of Kearney, the toothpick munching scoundrel
who made the right choice to spare Miss Sinclair;
Alberto, Paolino, lovable clowns;
Brothers ABC, I have no ill will—
and, if you care, I'll share a small secret:
I enjoyed Angus, Brogan, and Connell
and their antics, likely more than I should;
Stanislaw Krakowski who did not shirk
when confronted with much danger and risk;
and Smokey the cat, who salvaged the day.
I have cherished them all in the last year,
and see them so clearly that at odd times
I believe, for a moment, they are real—
and when the thought passes and I awake
from my writer's creative reverie,
brief and diaphanous though it might be,
I mourn the loss of characters I love
who only live within my fleeting thoughts.

Another peaceful night flowed from darkness to the new light of early morning, and—to the south, along the verdant ridges of Douglas Island—tattered edges of blue glowed between surging clouds floating serenely beyond the entrance to Gastineau Channel and high above the approaching steamship *Dolphin*. Abigail stood next to the now familiar hospital bed, the back of her left hand caressing Erik's sandy locks, the fingers of her right hand curled beneath the smooth-curved handle of the cane. Alberto Marino, taking his turn at guard duty so that Paolino could get some needed sleep in a real bed, slouched in his favorite hospital chair and tried to snooze without success. A puff of cool air fluttered the translucent curtains away from the open window.

Abigail felt the refreshing breath and turned to watch the fragile curtains float away from the window frame. "When does Paolino return?"

Alberto answered without opening his eyes. "My brother returns at ten. Then I shall walk to the house on Third Street and sleep in a real bed too, until after the noon."

Abigail limped to the window and pulled the curtain aside. "I can see blue sky down the channel. Looks like we shall be graced by another lovely day."

Alberto stretched upright to see better through the open window. "Yes, I can see the blue sky also. It is true that today is a good day."

Abigail released the curtain, shuffled along the wall, and lowered herself into the chair with difficulty. "But I would pray for a lifetime of rain if I thought it would mean that Erik would awaken."

Alberto frowned and then giggled. "A lifetime of rain? I think your prayer is almost answered now."

Abigail smiled: the first time in three days. "You know what I mean, Alberto."

Alberto returned the smile. "Yes, Miss Abigail Sinclair. I know very well what you mean."

———

Returning from a trip to the steamship dock to check on a long anticipated but still not arrived parcel from Italy, Paolino Marino crutch-walked up Gold Street on his way to the St. Ann's Hospital at the corner of Fifth and Gold. He scampered past the Third Street intersection and waved at the woman who owned the home of his present convalescence. She waved back then pinned a pair of cotton bloomers over a drooping clothesline. Excited by the news he had just learned, he quickened his pace and the length of his two-legged stride. He arrived at Fourth Street nearly breathless, but plunged ahead with constant speed until the St. Ann's Hospital came into view. He pivoted left at Fifth Street and nearly fell when a crutch tip caught in a knot hole. He regained his balanced and held pace to the front door of the hospital. He almost fell again as he hop-skipped up the stairs to Erik Meyer's room. When he burst into the room and lifted the crutches in the air, he could barely speak between panting breaths.

"Miss Abigail...and my...brother! I have news! I have news! News...of things...you do not...know!"

Abigail, alarmed by Paolino's unnatural exuberance, jumped from her chair. "Paolino. What in heaven's sake is going on? Are you drunk?"

Alberto, afraid that his brother might fall without the crutches, leaped across the room to catch him. "Paolino. Indeed what is wrong? Are you a problem?"

Paolino stabbed the crutches to the floor and began pacing. "No, no, no, my...friends. I feel fine. But...I have news you...do not understand."

Abigail stepped forward. "What news do you bring, Paolino, that has excited you so?"

Paolino slid into a chair and waited until he could speak without gasping. "The news is this. I am at the steamship dock, looking for my package from home—and I should tell you that it has arrived not—and I find Miss Marie Prideaux instead of the package."

Alberto smirked. "That is no news, my foolish brother. Miss Prideaux can be found at the steamship dock before."

Abigail stiffened at the name. "Just so, Paolino. That does not sound like news at all."

Paolino grinned. "But today you are wrong, my friends. I spoke with Miss Prideaux for many minutes, and she is leaving on the steamer south today, and not to return forever."

Abigail's green eyes widened. "Leaving? But why would she leave?"

Paolino leaned the crutches against the wall. "That is the funny story. She is leaving because Erik was thought dead. She read of it in the newspaper, and believed it of the truth. She did not know Erik sleeps in this room with us. She thought he was gone. But still she is leaving."

Abigail slumped into the chair. "Oh my. That really is news."

"I told you I had the news, but you did not think so. Now I think you do."

Alberto responded, "I forgive you, my brother. I did not believe you either until now…" then added, "…but this is good news, Miss Abigail, because now you have Erik alone, and do not need to worry of Miss Prideaux much more."

Abigail paused. "I suppose that is true. I've only to sit in this chair and do nothing at all, and I will have Erik all to myself."

Paolino answered. "Yes. There is nothing for you to do. Just stay here in the chair and Mister Erik will have no choice but to love you. This is news. Wonderful news."

Abigail sat motionless. "Yes, he *will* have no choice, I suppose."

Alberto returned to his chair. "Then we shall all sit here in the chairs and do nothing, and Erik will love you instead, and this will make us happy."

The three conspirators sat in the uncomfortable wooden hospital chairs without talking. Alberto and Paolino both shifted position several times, but Abigail did not move. The window curtain fluttered again. An eagle squawked somewhere to the north, beyond the edge of town. A squirrel chattered in a tree near the front of the hospital. Alberto glanced at his watch. Paolino drummed three fingers on the arm of his uncomfortable chair. Abigail did not move. The floor outside Erik's room creaked when a nurse walked by. Someone coughed in the next room. Paolino stopped drumming his fingers and began tapping his foot. Abigail did not move. A dog barked several blocks away, somewhere on Third Street. Children screamed in the next yard as they played a game of tag. Alberto held the watch up to his ear and listened to the tick...tick...tick of the tiny watch gears. Abigail did not move. Paolino stopped tapping his foot and resumed the previous drumming pattern with his fingers. Alberto closed the watch and returned it to his pocket. Down at the steamship dock, the whistle of the steamer *Dolphin* shrilled, signaling departure within the hour.

Abigail stood and adjusted her sling. "I have to go, my beloved friends."

Alberto jumped with surprise. "Where do you go?"

"To the steamship dock, to tell Marie Prideaux that Erik Meyer is alive."

Paolino stood without his crutches. "But why, Miss Abigail? Why? I thought you loved Mister Erik with your big heart. You just have to do nothing."

Abigail soughed. "I do, Paolino, I do love him. And it is because I love him that I must find Marie and tell her the truth. I have little time to find her, so I must hurry to the task."

Abigail rushed across the room, her cane tapping quickly along the hardwood floor. Full of haste, she slammed the door vigorously after stepping into the hallway. Alberto and Paolino listened to the cane's fading echo as it tap-tap-tapped down the stairs and through the front door.

Erik Meyer opened his eyes at the sound of the slamming door. He turned his head and squinted at the blurred images of Alberto and Paolino for several minutes before speaking. "What has happened? Is she here? You must tell me. Is she?"

The Marino brothers fell against the side of the hospital bed. Alberto spoke first. "My friend, you have come back. You have come back. We are so happy now. You are good again."

"Is she here? I must talk to her. I must."

Paolino spoke next. "No, Mister Erik. She is not here, but Miss Abigail has run to fetch her now. You will speak with her soon. Very soon."

"But it is Abigail that I must speak to. I must tell her that I love her before it is too late."

Confused, Paolino answered, "But I thought you speak of Marie, my friend."

Erik Meyer tried to push himself up, but fell back into the bed. "Thank God she is safe. Thank God. I love her so, my lovely Abigail. Thank God."

Paolino snatched Alberto's sleeve and yanked. "I would go, but you are the fast one now. You must run and catch Miss Abigail a second time, my brother. Run! Catch her soon. Run! Run!

———

Abigail, her legs aching and her shoulder throbbing, spotted Marie Prideaux sitting on a large trunk, waiting to board the steamer *Dolphin*. Abigail slowed her pace to calm her breathing as she walked up to Marie.

Marie looked up, startled. "Miss Sinclair. How nice to see you again before I depart."

Abigail leaned on the cane. "Good morning to you, Miss Prideaux. I have something to confess, and I believe it will change your mind about leaving."

Marie smiled. "Why, Miss Sinclair—whatever could that be?"

Abigail breathed deeply. "Erik Meyer is alive."

Marie smiled. "Yes, I know. Isn't it wonderful."

"You know? But how?"

"Paolino Marino told me of Erik, not more than an hour ago."

"And you are still leaving? But Erik loves you, and I thought that you loved him."

Marie stood and gently grasped Abigail's cane hand. "When Paolino told me that Erik Meyer was alive, I nearly decided to stay. I really did. He is such a good and honest man. But Paolino also told me of your great devotion to Erik. I must therefore share with you, Abigail, that the late Ulrich Boucher had already ranted of your unrequited love, so I also must confess that I was not unaware of it."

Abigail sniffed. "Even so, why are you are still leaving? What of Erik? What of his love for you? Is that not reason enough to stay?"

Marie smiled and patted Abigail's hand. "One might think so, especially someone of your genuine heart. But I have realized in the last few days that I can never give myself completely to any one man, not even a man as good as Erik Meyer. My departure today may be the only good and true thing I have done since my arrival in Juneau."

"But Erik…."

"Abigail, do not argue with me on this. Erik deserves better than me. He deserves much better. He deserves you."

Tears pooled around Abigail's green eyes and streamed down her gentle cheeks. "I do not think that Erik loves me in the way you think, Marie."

"Oh, I wouldn't fret about that. I believe that he loves you more deeply than you can imagine. He just doesn't realize it yet. But he will. He will."

Skittering to a stop and gasping heavily, Alberto Marino nearly plunged headlong into Marie and Abigail. "Miss Abigail. Miss Abigail. I have caught you at last."

"Alberto—what is it?"

"Miss Abigail. I have news!"

# Epilogue

*Treadwell Complex*

The mines of Douglas Island and the Treadwell Complex—Ready Bullion, Mexican, 700 Foot, and Treadwell itself—continued to thrive after Marie's departure from Juneau in 1899. Open pit mining, which had begun to decline in 1886, ceased entirely in 1906. You can still see the largest of these open pits, the Treadwell Glory Hole,[27] if you are willing to hike the one-mile trail from Sandy Beach at the south end of Douglas. The glory hole reached 1,700 feet long by 420 feet across by 450 feet deep before the miners finished with it.

Controversy thrived as well. In the spring of 1907 the miners declared a general strike and nearly 800 men walked off the job. At the request of acting governor William L. Driston, 54 soldiers were shipped in from Fort William H. Seward to quell any riots. The strike ended on April 20th, but a little more than a year later another strike erupted in May 1908 and did not end until four months had passed. Because of strikes and other labor problems, the Alaska Treadwell Gold Mining Company eventually refused to hire men who held membership cards in the Western Federation of Miners Labor Union.

Technological innovations flourished during the early 1900s. Under the leadership of F.W. Bradley, all steam-operated hoists and mining equipment were converted to run on more efficient electric power. A seasonal hydroelectric plant and flume were constructed at Thane in 1910. With adequate water, this plant could generate more than 2,200 kilowatts of electrical power. Power lines crossed the

101

Gastineau Channel on their way to Treadwell about where the Juneau-Douglas Bridge is now located. The Nugget Creek Powerhouse, also seasonal, was built near the base of the Mendenhall Glacier in 1914, and with peak water flow could produce 2,300 kilowatts of electrical power. The central steam power plant was ultimately enlarged in 1914 to provide electrical power to all of the mines during the winter months when the seasonal hydroelectric plants were not operating.

On April 20, 1917—after years of allowing the pillars left in the stopes to collapse without providing an alternate supporting structure—the ground subsided beneath the Treadwell Natatorium and the steam-heated water drained from the 30 by 70 foot pool tank. Early the next evening, around 6:30 pm, water began seeping through the sand beneath the natatorium and disappearing. Some time before 11:00 pm sea water from Gastineau Channel began pouring into a large hole that had formed under the fire hall. By 12:40 am the following morning the last of the miners were brought up from the 2,100-foot level of Treadwell Mine as sea water continued to pour in. By 1:15 am the natatorium and fire hall disappeared into the collapsing hole. At 2:15 am a salt water geyser exploded 200 feet above the shaft head frame signaling that the Treadwell, Mexican, and 700-Foot Mines were completely flooded. All of the mules, horses, and mining machinery were lost in the cave-in and subsequent flood. A concrete bulkhead, constructed in 1913 at the only level connecting with the other mines, saved the Ready Bullion Mine from a similar disaster.

### Alaska Gastineau Mining Company

The age of the Alaska Gastineau Mining Company began in 1911 when it was incorporated under the laws of the State of New York. In 1912, General Manager Bartlett L. Thane[28] developed a plan to construct a hydroelectric plant at Salmon Creek (6,000 horsepower); a 6,000-ton mill at Sheep Creek on Gastineau Channel; 3-1/2 miles of railroad tracks between the inland Perseverance Mine and the planned Sheep Creek mill; and all living quarters, warehouses, stores, and other support facilities as required. His construction schedule indicated completion of the entire project by January 1, 1915.

To provide adequate reservoir storage and a year-round water source (the first in Juneau) for the hydroelectric power plant, the first true constant-angle arch dam measuring 168 feet high and 648 feet across was built across Salmon Creek. Construction began in July 1913 and was completed less than a year later.[29] The concrete dam tapered from 47.5 feet at the base to a mere 6 feet at the top, and, because the double arch design creates only compressive forces, no reinforcing steel was used during construction. The project included two powerhouses: one about a mile below the dam and one on Gastineau Channel. Train tracks connected the power houses to facilitate the transport of men, equipment, and supplies. The Salmon Creek Dam is still in use today, and you can trek up the hill to view it, if you have the inclination and vigor.

In November 1912, approximately eight months before laborers poured the first concrete for the dam, construction began on the Sheep Creek Adit, a 10-foot by 8-foot tunnel bored through Mt. Roberts to connect the inland Perseverance Mine with the mill on Gastineau Channel. Construction of this passageway, nearly 10,500 feet long and sloped at a constant two-percent grade, progressed at an average rate of 544 feet per month, a world's record at the time. Crews of 70 men working in three shifts completed the adit in April 1914. The main shaft of the Perseverance Mine extended 1,530 feet deep through nine levels. The Sheep Creek Railway connected the mill to the adit portal, and then continued on through the adit to the Perseverance Mine main shaft. The total distance from the mill to the main shaft was 3-1/2 miles and, at a top speed of 12 miles per hour, could be traversed by electric locomotives pulling 40-car ore trains in a little more than three hours.

Construction of the Alaska Gastineau Mining Company mill on Gastineau Channel progressed as well, and by November 1915 the mill had reached full operation processing 6,000 tons of ore a day. Below the great mill a wharf with three warehouses, shops, offices, a combination clubhouse and dining room that could serve 500 in a single sitting, six 50-man boarding houses, three and four-room family cottages, and other support facilities spread along the water's edge.[30]

After an initial period of stunning success, technical problems with the grade of ore, manpower shortages brought on by America's entrance into World War I, inadequate prices of gold relative to required profit, and difficulties processing ore wetted by surface run-off flooding into caved stopes forced the Alaska Gastineau Mining Company to cease operations in June 1921, a mere six years after full operation had commenced. In an effort to salvage some gain from the venture, Bart Thane pursued the idea of a pulp mill at Thane for seven years, but without success. Discouraged, he began drinking, and, while in New York trying to find a buyer for the property, he contracted pneumonia. He died at the age of 49 in November 1927.

### Alaska Juneau Gold Mining Company

Incorporated under the laws of the State of West Virginia in 1897, the A.J. Gold Mining Company achieved new leadership in 1900 when Frederick Worthen Bradley (the same F.W. Bradley of our story) purchased a large share of the company and became president later in the same year. In the late 1800s and early 1900s the mining operation consisted primarily of open pits and a 30-stamp mill located in the Silver Bow Basin. Set up in 1896, the mill could process up to 150 tons of ore each day if operated continuously.

In 1903 and again in 1905, adits were driven between 400 and 500 feet below the open pits in Silver Bow Basin to explore the extent and quality of ore. Samples indicated a relatively low grade of ore—90 cents of gold per ton of ore at the time—and the possibility of a very large ore body, if deep enough. To prove sufficient depth, F.W. Bradley took a financial risk in 1910 and contracted to bore a tunnel deep under the ore body. Construction commenced in November 1911, and over the next two years a tunnel 9-feet high by 7-feet wide was driven a little more than 6,500 feet into Mt. Roberts. A shaft was bored near the end of the tunnel and extended 800 feet vertically until it broke through the surface near the original 30-stamp mill.

Bradley devised a plan to construct four mills of 150-stamps each on the hillside above Gastineau Channel to process up to 8,000 tons of ore per day. Although similar in appearance to the Alaska Gastineau Mining Company mill at Sheep Creek, the A.J. facility would use ball mills instead of tube mills.[31] The huge mill began construction in 1916 and became fully operational in March 1917. A steam power plant was also constructed in 1916, and, its diesel boilers fueled from two 55,000-barrel storage tanks located on the waterfront, could generate 8,000 kilowatts of electrical power.

An now the story gets interesting. After the facility began milling operations on March 31, 1917, it achieved a dismal average of only 1,200 tons per day, miserably short of the anticipated 8,000 tons per day. Remember the decision to use ball instead of tube mills? Well, that turned out to be a problem. The ball mills, used to fine-grind the ore after it passed through crushers, had demonstrated success grinding copper ore in Arizona but had never been tested in Juneau. The ore mined from Silver Bow Basin turned out to be much harder than copper ore, and the crushers delivered a product that was too coarse to allow efficient fine-grinding by the ball mills. Extensive finger pointing ensued, and the chief consulting engineer, J.H. MacKenzie, took most of the blame and resigned at the end of May 1917. Although the mill's capacity gradually increased to around 3,200 tons per day by December, the company continued to operate at a loss.

F.W. Bradley personally supervised a massive redesign and renovation effort, and actually paid for the cost from his own funds until the company issued $3,500,000 in bonds in 1919. The crushing units preceding the problematic ball mills were rearranged and increased in quantity until they could deliver sufficiently-fine-crushed ore. Production improved, but then other technical problems emerged. The Alaska Juneau Gold Mining Company operated at a loss (it did make a small profit in 1924) until 1928 when, after running for 363 days, it achieved a profit of more than $3.3 million.

The A.J. Company reached its acme in the late 1930s, employing more than 1,000 men 24-hours a day in three shifts every day of the year save the Fourth of July and Christmas. Juneau restaurants, movie houses, and bars remained open 24-hours a day as well to cater to the miners. The A.J. mine achieved its last profitable year in 1941. In early October 1942 the War Production Board issued an order to shut down all non-essential mines to release men for the war effort. Company officials decided to continue operation at a break-even point with only 350 men rather than shut down. However, demands by the local union for a wage increase, and consequent approval of a 14-cents per hour raise by the War Labor Board in 1943, pushed the mine to the financial breaking point and the A.J. ceased operations in early April 1944.

During its nearly 30 years of operation, the A.J. Mine processed more than 90 million tons of rock and ore and produced in excess of $80 million in gold. No other mining company has ever mined such low-grade ore underground for so long and made a profit. On March 20, 1965, a raging fire gutted the great mill building and the Alaska Juneau Gold Mining Company—and the heroic era of gold mining in Juneau, Douglas, and Treadwell—effectively came to an end.[32]

# Resources

I used the following resources during the writing of portions of this novella. I am deeply indebted to the organizations, authors, and their excellent work.

Alaska's Digital Archives, a collaborative effort initiated by the Rasmuson Library at the University of Alaska Fairbanks, the Consortium Library at the University of Alaska Anchorage, and the Alaska State Library in Juneau, http://vilda.alaska.edu/index.php.

Roppel, Patricia. *Southeast Alaska - A Pictorial History*, published by The Donning Company, Copyright 1983 by Patricia Roppel.

Stone, David and Brenda. *Hard Rock Gold...The Story of the Great Mines that were the Heartbeat of Juneau*, published by the Juneau Centennial Committee, 1980, Copyright by David and Brenda Stone.

Mahaffy, Charlotte L. *I Remember Treadwell*, published by the Gastineau Channel Historical Society, 1992.

# Photo Credits

Page 11: Establishment of the Russian-American Company at Norfolk, Sitka Sound, Alaska, 1805. (Alaska State Library, Alaska Purchase Centennial Collection, G.H. von Langsdorff, ASL-P20-142)

Page 16: View from Mexican head frame showing part of Treadwell with Douglas City and Juneau in the distance. (Alaska State Library, Case & Draper Collection, Case & Draper, ASL-P39-0956)

Page 22: Douglas, Alaska, 1908. St. Ann's Hospital. (Alaska State Library, Case & Draper Collection, W. H. Case, ASL-P39-1021)

Page 27: Schooner Helga Caroline in Juneau, Alaska, ca. 1894. (Alaska State Library, Winter & Pond Collection, Winter & Pond, ASL-P87-0778)

Page 33: One way from Douglas to Treadwell 1899. Photograph of rails running along the waterfront in front of wooden houses, with cedar canoes on snow-covered beach. Abigail's house is the second one from the right, and that might be her walking in the distance, but you'll have to decide for yourself. (Alaska State Library, Alaska State Library Place File Collection, ASL-P01-0965)

Page 37: Ballaine's huge Cat with its prominent tail. This photograph was taken in Fairbanks in 1896. I have no idea who Ballaine was, but the cat looks like my cat (his name is Smokey too) and since I needed a cat character to make the story work, why not use the image of my own cat? However, I feel compelled to share with you that when I showed this picture to Kris (my wife), she said, "That's just a plain black cat with some white. Smokey's a Snowshoe Siamese and much more beautiful. Maybe so, but I couldn't find a picture of a damn Snowshoe Siamese in the Alaska Digital Archives, so this is close enough. (University of Alaska Fairbanks, Gordon Picotte Photograph Collection, Gordon Picotte, UAF-1986-189-10)

Page 44: Auditorium Treadwell Club. Treadwell, Alaska. The photograph is not dated, but the collection time period is indicated as ca. 1890-1920. (Alaska State Library, William R. Norton Collection, W.H. Case, ASL-P226-331)

Page 48: Treadwell Alaska. July 4th, 1908. A celebration occurred in Douglas on the same date. (Alaska State Library, William R. Norton Collection, W.H. Case, ASL-P226-305)

Page 55: Treadwell Mine, 1500 ft. leavel [level] Ready Bullion. This photograph was taken in 1908. (Alaska State Library, Juliane Nick Dexter Photograph Collection, W.H. Case, ASL-P40-21)

Page 61: Treadwell Store. A specific date is not given, but the time period is 1896 to 1913. (Alaska State Library, Case & Draper Collection, Case & Draper, ASL-P39-1142)

Page 66: A crew surveying the lot lines following the Louvre fire on Front Street, ca. 1908. (Alaska State Library, Winter & Pond Collection, Winter & Pond, ASL-P87-1050)

Page 72: Third St. Juneau, Alaska. Looking down on Third and Gold Streets, with wooden streets and sidewalks. U.S. Courthouse in far background. A specific date is not given, but the time period is 1896 to 1913. (Alaska State Library, Skinner Foundation Collection, Frank H. Nowell, ASL-P44-03-022)

Page 80: Treadwell Mine, Supt. Residence and Machine Shop. View looking toward Juneau and Mayflower Island in 1908. (Alaska State Library, Juliane Nick Dexter Photograph Collection, Case & Draper, ASL-P40-16)

Page 88: St. Anne's Hospital. Juneau, Alaska. (Alaska State Library, William R. Norton Collection, W. H. Case, ASL-P226-227)

Page 96: A.S.S. Co. Str. *Dolphin*. Juneau, Alaska. Aug. 19, 1905. (Alaska State Library, William R. Norton Collection, Case & Draper, ASL-P226-624)

Page 105: Alaska Juneau mill fire, 3/20/1965. (Alaska State Library, Robert N. DeArmond Photograph Collection, R. N. DeArmond, ASL-P258-III-0745)

Page 113: Six men, with John Treadwell seated second from

right. (Alaska State Library, Louis L. Stein Collection, Edward De-Groff, ASL-P172-16a)

Page 115: Battery Floor, A.T.G.M. Co's. "300 Mill," Douglas Island c. 1899. (Alaska State Library, Winter & Pond Collection, Winter & Pond, ASL-P87-0376)

Page 116: Group of men posing outside the Juneau City Hotel. (Alaska State Library, George Family Collection, ASL-P344-099)

Page 117: Juneau Hotel built in the 1890s to replace the Juneau City Hotel on 2nd Street, it burned down in September 1911. (Alaska State Library, Winter & Pond Collection, Winter & Pond, ASL-P87-0952)

Page 118: Showing A. S. S. Co. dock and P. C. Co. addition, ca. 1917. Alaska Steamship Co. and Pacific Coast Co. docks at center. Chlopeck No. 3 at dock. Ferry dock in foreground with ferries Teddy, Lone Fisherman, and Amy. Sign in image: Juneau Ferry and Navigation Co., Boat Leaves Juneau-Douglas-Treadwell (giving departure times). (Alaska State Library, Winter & Pond Collection, Winter & Pond, ASL-P87-0856)

Page 119: Treadwell Express 1908. If you squint your eyes, you can almost see Abigail's canvas-covered steamer trunk. (Alaska State Library, William R. Norton Collection, W.H. Case, ASL-P226-334)

Page 120: Treadwell Miners 1908. (Alaska State Library, William R. Norton Collection, W.H. Case, ASL-P226-339)

Page 120: Treadwell boarding house (Alaska). Main dining room July 4th 1908. (Alaska State Library, Case & Draper Collection, W.H. Case, ASL-P39-0994)

Page 121: Juneau Alaska, July 4th, 1907. The punctuation is as appears on the title of the photograph. Note the five clarinets (front row) but no saxophones. (Alaska State Library, William R. Norton Collection, Case & Draper, ASL-P226-182)

Page 121: Machine shops co. #4. Hose race. July 4th 1908. Treadwell, Alaska. Note that my reference to "striped shirts" in the story is historically accurate. (Alaska State Library, William R. Norton Collection, W. H. Case, ASL-P226-302)

Page 122: General view of Treadwell Gold Mines, Alaska, c. 1899. The description on the photograph reads: Treadwell Hoisting Works, 240-Stamp Mill and Coal Bunkers. Douglas Island, Alaska, c. 1899. (Alaska State Library, Winter & Pond Collection, Winter & Pond, ASL-P87-0333)

Page 123: Treadwell machine shop—looking south. This is Connell's view as he tees up at the north end of the machine shop. (Alaska State Library, William R. Norton Collection, Case & Draper, ASL-P226-320)

Page 124: Treadwell Glory Hole, c. 1910. (Alaska State Library, Winter & Pond Collection, Winter & Pond, ASL-P87-0350)

Page 124: Bartlett L. Thane seated at desk in office. Photograph was taken in Juneau, Alaska and is undated. (Alaska State Library, Winter & Pond Collection, Winter & Pond, ASL-P87-2398)

Page 125: Dam construction site, Salmon Creek (Alaska State Library, Alaska Electric Light & Power Company Photograph Collection, Winter & Pond, ASL-P140-017)

Page 126: Plant of Alaska Gastineau Mining Co. at Thane. Photograph taken in 1917. (University of Alaska Anchorage, Archives and Special Collections, National Geographic Society Katmai Expeditions Photograph, Robert F. Griggs, UAA-hmc-0186-volume3-1022)

Page 127: Overview of A.J. Mill. (Alaska State Library, Alaska Juneau Gold Mining Company Records, asl-m999-AJ-Mill-003)

# End Notes

1: This date is taken from *Hard Rock Gold*. The booklet *I Remember Treadwell* claims that French Pete staked the Paris Lode in November 1881.

2: John Treadwell sold his interest in the Alaska Treadwell Gold Mining Company in June 1889. He died penniless in 1927. John Treadwell is the man with the moustache and hat (second from the right).

3: *Hard Rock Gold* notes on page 10 that John Treadwell, John Fry, and James Freeborn initially each owned a third interest in any claims staked by Treadwell, and that the three partners organized the Alaska Mill and Mining Company in 1882. Although a copy of the articles of incorporation are included on page 11, there is no mention of the Alaska Treadwell Gold Mining Company until page 13 when you find out that John Treadwell sold his interests to the recently incorporated Treadwell Company in 1889, and that the company had previously financed the Alaska Mexican Gold Mining Company and the Alaska United Gold Mining Company. The City and Borough of Juneau website (www.juneau.lib.ak.us/history/treadwel.php) provided additional clarification of the Treadwell Company's 1889 buyout of all investors, including Treadwell, for $4,000,000.

4: From *The American Heritage Dictionary*: Glengarry - A woolen cap that is creased lengthwise and often has short ribbons at the back. [After Glengarry, a valley of central Scotland.]

5: The steamship *Willapa* actually arrived in Juneau on its maiden voyage in March 1885, but I liked the photo of the ship, and the name, and decided to fictionalize the first arrival to 1899. I offer my humblest apology to any readers who are history purists.

6: The peak of Mount Roberts rises 3,819 feet above sea level (1,164 meters).

7: Captain Larsen's description of the Treadwell Complex is based on selected photos from the Alaska State Library Digital Archives and the "Surface Map of Treadwell" on page 30 of *Hard Rock Gold*. The map is dated 1914, so you will have to trust that I did my best, given that many of the photos were not dated, to accurately describe how Treadwell Complex might have appeared to Abigail as she cruised down Gastineau Channel in 1899.

8: According to *I Remember Treadwell*, the Treadwell Club building was actually built in 1903. Interestingly, I found a photo of the interior of the Treadwell Natatorium in the Alaska State Library Digital Archives dated circa 1900. I can't imagine that they built the swimming pool first, but who really knows?

9: Finally (and, I must admit, by coincidence), a date that aligns perfectly with the chronology of my story. The Treadwell 300-stamp mill was, in truth, built in 1899, and was, in truth, the largest mill of its kind in the world. If you don't believe me, see *Hard Rock Gold*, page 13. However, please don't expect this level of accuracy from here on out. Below is a photo of the interior of the mill taken in 1899, the year of construction.

10: In the Alaska State Library Digital Archives I found a photograph titled "Douglas, Alaska, 1908" (see page 22) which shows a woman and three children standing in front of the multi-story "St. Ann's Hospital on St. Ann's St." The Victoria, BC Sisters of St. Ann website (www.sistersofsaintanne.org/bc) indicates that the first St. Ann's Hospital was built in Juneau in 1886 before a second was constructed in Douglas in 1895.

11: According to *Hard Rock Gold* (page 17) Frederick Worthen Bradley actually arrived in Juneau in 1900—I warned you not to expect perfect accuracy. Initially he served as president of the Alaska Juneau Gold Mining Company, but became president of Treadwell in 1911. An engineer with special expertise in low-cost mining, his previous experience included mines in Nevada County, California, and the Coeur d'Alene district of Idaho. He was in his office in San Francisco at the time of the Treadwell Cave-In in 1917.

12: The Juneau Hotel was built in the 1890s to replace the Juneau City Hotel on 2nd Street. It was indeed located between the Windsor Saloon and the *Alaska Searchlight* newspaper as described by Erik Meyer to Abigail. Photos of both hotels are included because I know you are wondering what they looked like. The Juneau Hotel is on the next page, as you might have already guessed from the modern storefront glazing system.

13: Built in 1898 for the Juneau Ferry and Navigation Company, the 72-foot steamer *Flosie* primarily transported passengers and mail between Juneau, Haines, and Skagway. However, it is very possible that it also ferried passengers between Juneau, Treadwell, and Douglas. Below is a photo of the Alaska Steamship Co. and Pacific Coast Co. Juneau docks in 1917, with three ferries in the foreground. Although not historically of the exact time of Abigail's first ferry passage from Juneau to Treadwell, it does gives you an idea of the maritime ambiance of the period.

14: Sough is an intransitive verb of chiefly Scottish and Northern English origins. It means to make a soft murmuring or rustling sound. Now that you've improved your vocabulary, it will please you to know what it means when I use the word again.

15: As explained by Captain Larsen in the third chapter (Voyage), the narrow-gage tracks connected all of the Treadwell Complex facilities and even extended to the sawmill in Douglas. Next is a photograph of the narrow gage tracks and train taken in 1908.

16: The Treadwell boarding house, as Erik described to Abigail, was located on the waterfront south of the Treadwell wharf. The photograph below was taken in 1908, but the boarding house probably existed prior to 1900. Erik Meyer is standing in the back row, 12th from the left. I also found an intriguing photograph of the main dining room taken on July 4, 1908, with hundreds of miners dressed in suits and ties for the holiday feast. I tried to count them, but the severe perspective defeated me.

17: Yes, the Treadwell Club had an official band, and I have assumed that their repertoire included a wind ensemble arrangement of the Blue Danube Waltz. In the 1907 photograph below, the band poses in Juneau on a board street in front of downtown offices.

18: According to *Hard Rock Gold*, each of the four Treadwell mines had its own fire department. Below, the Machine Shops Co. #4 fire department prepares for the July 4, 1908 hose races in Treadwell.

19: It took me a long time to find this, so I insist on telling you about it. In the late 1800s (I could not verify the exact year), the first woman dancer competed against the men in the Highland Games. Her name was Jenny Douglas, and she evidently created a sensation when she stepped onto the competition platform dressed in kilt, doublet, plaid, and sporran—just like the men. The judges allowed her to compete because they could find no rule against it. Today, the vast majority of Highland Dancing competitors are women.

20: By studying both the photograph below and the map of Treadwell in *Hard Rock Gold*, I determined that the Treadwell Hoisting Works is comprised of the two tall buildings to the left. This is where miners gained access to the vertical shaft leading to the different levels of the mine. The photograph below was taken in 1899, the same year as Abigail's arrival.

21: Simply put, a stope is an excavation, and stoping is the act of excavating. Stoping involves leaving part of the broken ore for an excavation platform and to support the ceiling and walls. At Treadwell, the stopes (excavations) were driven horizontally from vertical shafts approximately every 200 feet. Stopes averaged 60 to 100 feet wide, and were created by drilling and blasting. See *Hard Rock Gold*, page 17, for additional technical information.

22: Muck is ore or rock that has been broken by blasting.

23: I have made assumptions concerning the available medical technology in Treadwell in 1899. However, just so you don't doubt the rigor of my research, Dr. William Stewart Halsted (born in New York in 1852) pioneered the use of cocaine as an injectable anesthetic in 1884. The first synthetic local anesthetic, procaine (better known by its trade name Novocain), was developed in 1905. Oh, I almost forgot—Dr. Halsted also pioneered the use of rubber gloves during surgical procedures.

24: There is no historical evidence that dynamite was ever manufactured in Treadwell, but it could have happened, and that's good enough for me. And, since I expect you will ask later, Alfred Nobel invented dynamite in 1866. It is made by combining three parts nitroglycerine, one part diatomaceous earth, and a small admixture of sodium carbonate. Although highly sensitive to physical shock, nitroglycerine can be desensitized by cooling it to its freezing point, a relatively warm (in Juneau) 50 degrees Fahrenheit.

25: The *Daily Alaska Dispatch* commenced business in Juneau and Douglas in 1899. Its name was changed to the *Alaska Dispatch* (Seattle) in 1919. Other Alaska newspapers available in Juneau in 1899 included the *Alaska Truth, Sunday Sun, Alaska Mining Record,* and the *Fort Wrangell News.*

26: I thought I should share my inspiration for this scene with you. Below is Connell's view of the Treadwell Machine Shop as he tees up. Fore!

27: More than five million tons of ore were removed from the Treadwell Glory Hole, creating an impressive pit that is still visible today. The photo below is dated c. 1910.

28: Below is a photograph of Bartlett L. Thane. He is seated at his desk in Juneau, Alaska. Note the map of the Alaska Gastineau Mining Company holdings at Thane and the Perseverance Mine displayed on the wall behind. Take a close look at that phone too.

29: The Salmon Creek Dam was constructed in 1913 and 1914, and required less than a year to complete. *Hard Rock Gold* states on page 40 that the dam is 175 feet high. I have used 168 feet from the Alaska Digital Archives in the text.

30: The Alaska Gastineau Mining Company mill on Gastineau Channel in 1917. It was located four miles southeast of Juneau at the site of present-day Thane.

31: I read the description of tube and ball mills three times in the footnote on page 61 of *Hard Rock Gold*, and studied the photograph on page 62 for more than five minutes, and still don't think I can adequately describe the technical differences. Let's just say that tube mills use large tubes filled with pebbles to crush the ore, and ball mills use smaller tubes filled with steel balls to crush the ore.

32: I thought it fitting that I should conclude with a photograph of the A.J. Gold Mine in its glory days. Thank you for reading *Heart of Abigail*. I truly appreciate it.